ACCA

PRACTICE & REVISION KIT

Paper 2.3

Business Taxation

FA 2004

For June 2005 and December 2005 exams

BPP Professional Education
January 2005

First edition April 2001
Fifth edition January 2005

ISBN 0 7517 2175 1 (previous edition 0 7517 1557 3)

British Library Cataloguing-in-Publication Data
A catalogue record for this book
is available from the British Library

Published by

BPP Professional Education
Aldine House, Aldine Place
London W12 8AW

www.bpp.com

Printed in Great Britain by Ashford Colour Press

We are grateful to the Association of Chartered Certified Accountants for
permission to reproduce past examination questions. The answers to the past
examination questions have been prepared by BPP Professional Education.

CONTENTS

The headings indicate the main topics of questions, but questions often cover several different topics.

Preparation questions, listed in italics, are followed by guidance notes. These notes show you how to approach the question, and thus ease the transition from study to examination practice.

BPP PROFESSIONAL EDUCATION

BPP
PROFESSIONAL EDUCATION

BPP PROFESSIONAL EDUCATION

TOPIC INDEX

Listed below are the key Paper 2.3 syllabus topics and the numbers of the questions in this Kit covering those topics.

If you need to concentrate your practice and revision on certain topics or if you want to attempt all available questions that refer to a particular subject (be they preparation or exam-standard) you will find this index useful.

EFFECTIVE REVISION

What you must remember

Effective use of time as you approach the exam is very important. You must remember:

> **Believe in yourself**
> **Use time sensibly**

Believe in yourself

Are you cultivating the right attitude of mind? There is absolutely no reason why you should not pass this exam if you adopt the correct approach.

- **Be confident** – you've passed exams before, you can pass them again
- **Be calm** – plenty of adrenaline but no panicking
- **Be focused** – commit yourself to passing the exam

Use time sensibly
---

1   **How much study time do you have**? Remember that you must **eat, sleep,** and of course, **relax**.

2   **How will you split that available time between each subject?** A **revision timetable,** covering **what** and **how** you will revise, will help you organise your revision effectively.

3   **What is your learning style?** AM/PM? Little and often/long sessions? Evenings/weekends?

4   **Do you have quality study time?** Unplug the phone. Let everybody know that you're studying and shouldn't be disturbed.

5   **Are you taking regular breaks?** Most people absorb more if they do not attempt to study for long uninterrupted periods of time. A five minute break every hour (to make coffee, watch the news headlines) can make all the difference.

6   Are you **rewarding yourself** for your hard work? Are you leading a **healthy lifestyle**?

What to revise

Key topics

You need to spend most time on, and practise full questions on, **key topics**.

> Key topics
> - Recur regularly
> - Underpin whole paper
> - Appear often in compulsory questions
> - Discussed currently in press
> - Covered in recent articles by examiner
> - Shown as high priority in study material
> - Tipped by lecturer

Difficult areas

You may also still find certain areas of the syllabus difficult.

> Difficult areas
>
> - Areas you find dull or pointless
> - Subjects you highlighted as difficult when taking notes
> - Topics that gave you problems when you answered questions or reviewed the material

DON'T become depressed about these areas; instead do something about them.

- Build up your knowledge by **quick tests** such as the quick quizzes in your BPP Study Text.

- Work carefully through **numerical examples** and **questions** in the Text, and refer back to the Text if you struggle with computations in the Kit.

- **Note down weaknesses** that your answers to questions contained; you are less likely to make the same mistakes if you highlight where you went wrong.

Breadth of revision

Make sure your revision has sufficient **breadth**. You need to be able to answer both the compulsory questions and enough optional questions on the paper.

Paper 2.3

The key to passing this paper is to spend your time practising as many questions as possible. 40 of the 55 marks in Section A will cover computational techniques so you must make a good attempt at these to pass the paper.

How to revise

There are four main ways that you can revise a topic area.

Write it!
Read it!
Teach it!
Do it!

Write it!

The Course Notes and the Study Text are too bulky for revision. You need a slimmed down set of notes that summarise the key points. Writing important points down will help you recall them, particularly if your notes are presented in a way that makes it easy for you to remember them.

Read it!

You should read your notes or BPP Passcards actively, testing yourself by doing quick quizzes or writing summaries of what you have just read.

Teach it!

Exams require you to show your understanding. Teaching what you are revising to another person helps you practise explaining topics. Teaching someone who will challenge your understanding, someone for example who will be taking the same exam as you, can help both of you.

Do it!

Remember that you are revising in order to be able to answer questions in the exam. Answering questions will help you practise **technique** and **discipline**, which examiners emphasise over and over again can be crucial in passing or failing exams.

1   Start by attempting any **preparation questions** included for a particular syllabus area. These provide you with a firm foundation from which to attempt exam-standard questions.

2   The more exam-standard questions you do, the more likely you are to pass the exam. At the very least, you should attempt the **key questions** that are highlighted.

3   You should produce **full answers** under **timed conditions,** and don't cheat by looking at the answer! Look back at your notes or at your BPP Study Text instead if you are really struggling. Produce answer plans if you are running short of time.

4   Always read the **Tutor's hints** in the answers. They are there to help you, and will show you which points in the answer are the most important.

5   **Don't get despondent** if you didn't do very well. Refer to the **topic index** and try another question that covers the same subject.

6   When you think you can successfully answer questions on the whole syllabus, attempt the **two mock exams** at the end of the Kit. You will get the most benefit by sitting them under strict exam conditions, so that you gain experience of the four vital exam processes.

- Selecting questions
- Deciding on the order in which to attempt them
- Managing your time
- Producing answers

BPP's *Learning to Learn Accountancy* book gives further invaluable advice on how to approach revision.

BPP has also produced other vital revision aids.

- **Passcards** – Provide you with clear topic summaries and exam tips
- **Success tapes** – Help you revise on the move
- **i-Pass CDs** – Offer you tests of knowledge to be completed against the clock

You can purchase these products by completing the order form at the back of this Kit or by visiting www.bpp.com/acca.

REVISION PROGRAMME

Below is a suggested **step-by-step revision programme**. Please note that this is not the only approach – you may prefer to do your revision in a different order, and your college may suggest a different approach. However, **as a minimum you must do the key questions if you want to pass the exam.**

The BPP programme requires you to devote a **minimum of 25 hours** to revision of Paper 2.3. Any time you can spend over and above this should only increase your chances of success.

Suggested approach

1   For the topics covered in each revision period, **review** your notes and the relevant summaries in the **Paper 2.3 Passcards**.

2   Start by looking at the **preparation questions** for each topic. These questions are designed to easy the transition from study to exam standard questions. If you are very confident you may wish just to look through the answers to these questions. However, if you are not completely confident at tax attempt these questions properly.

3   Next do the **key questions** for that section. These are **shaded** in the table below, and, as we indicated earlier, are the questions you must attempt, even if you are short of time. Try to complete your answers without referring to our solutions.

4   For some questions we have suggested that you prepare **answer plans** rather than full solutions. This means that you should spend about 30% of the full time allowance for that question on brainstorming the question and drawing up a list of points to be included in an answer.

5   Once you have worked through all of the syllabus sections, **attempt both of the Mock Exams under strict exam conditions**. It is very important to practise doing these exams under exam conditions. Mock exam 2 includes questions on areas which BPP predicts will be examined in 2005.

Topic	2005 Passcard chapter	Questions in this kit	Comments	Done ✓
Revision period 1 *Schedule D Case I adjustments*				
Preparation questions	2	1, 2	Useful preparation questions. Produce answer plans if your time is limited.	
Key questions	2	3, 4	Answer these key questions in full. Note that in both questions it was important to give reasons for your adjustments.	

Revision programme

Topic	2005 Passcard chapter	Questions in this kit	Comments	Done ✓
Revision periods 2/3 *Computing corporation tax/Capital allowances*				
Preparation questions: computing corporation tax	1	5, 6, 7	Useful preparation questions to 'warm up' with. Question 7 covering long periods of account is particularly important. Questions 5 and 6 cover the new rule on distributions to non corporate shareholders. This is an important Finance Act 2004 change that could be considered a hot topic for the 2005 exams.	
Preparation question: capital allowances	3	10	Work through this question if your knowledge of capital allowances is rusty.	
Key questions: comprehensive computation	1, 2, 3, 4	8, 9, 11	Vitally important key questions that you must work through in full. These are similar to the compulsory questions that you will meet in Section A.	
Revision period 4 *Corporation tax losses*				
Preparation question	6	12	Straightforward preparation question. Work through the answer if you are short of time.	
Key question: single company losses	6	13	An important question covering a single company's losses. Answer in full.	
Preparation questions: group losses	7	20, 21	Useful questions. Work through the answers if your time is limited.	
Key question: group losses	7	22	Important question. Group losses are a popular exam question.	

(xii)

Topic	2005 Passcard chapter	Questions in this kit	Comments	Done ✓
Revision period 5 *Capital gains*				
Preparation question	5	14	Useful question. Work through the answer if your time is short.	
Key questions	5	15, 16	Useful questions. Answer in full. Question 16 is an example of how gains will be included in a longer corporate question. It is particularly important you can do this type of question.	
Revision period 6 *Overseas aspects (corporate)*				
Preparation question	8	17	Useful question. Work through the answer if time is short.	
Key questions	8	18, 19	Useful questions. Answer them in full.	
Revision period 7 *Self assessment for companies*				
Key question	9	23	If you are very short of time you could prepare an answer plan for this question.	
Revision period 8 *VAT*				
Preparation question	10, 11	24	Work through this answer quickly if time is short.	
Key questions	10, 11	25, 42	Useful questions. Answer in full. Question 3 of your paper will be a VAT question so it is worth being prepared for it.	
Revision period 9 *Income tax computations*				
Preparation questions	12, 16	34, 35	These are useful preparation questions but work through the answers if short of time.	

Revision programme

Topic	2005 Passcard chapter	Questions in this kit	Comments	Done ✓
Key questions	12, 16	36, 37, 38	Vitally important key questions. These are the types of income tax computation that will appear in Section A. Don't forget the time apportionment of benefits	
Revision period 10 *Employees*				
Preparation question: benefits	20	43	Useful question. Work through the answer if short of time.	
Key questions	19, 20, 21	44, 45	Useful questions. Answer in full. The computation of taxable benefits is frequently examined.	
Revision period 11 *Self-assessment for individuals/partnerships*				
Key questions	18	26, 27	Useful questions. Answer in full. You must practice answering written questions like this concisely. If you ramble through your answer you will overrun on time and the marker may find it hard to mark.	
Revision periods 12/13 *Schedule DI and trading losses for individuals*				
Key question: adjustment of profits	13	28	Key question that also includes basis period rules for an individual. Answer in full.	
Key questions: income tax losses	14	29, 30, 31	Useful key questions. Answer in full. The examiner considers losses to be a core topic. They may be examined in Section A or Section B of the exam.	

Topic	2005 Passcard chapter	Questions in this kit	Comments	Done ✓
Revision period 14				(xv)
Partnerships/Capital gains for individuals				
Preparation question: partnerships	15	32	This question is similar to the key question below so work through the answer if time is short. Note that you must allocate profits to each partner *before* working out what is assessed in each tax year.	
Key question: partnerships	15	33	Useful question. Answer in full. This is a standard partnership question.	
Preparation question: capital gains	17	39	Useful question. Remember that taper relief applies to individuals only.	
Key questions: capital gains	17	40, 41	Useful questions. Answer in full.	
Revision period 15/16				
Tax planning				
Remuneration packages	22	47	Key question. Answer in full.	
Employed v self employed	22	48	Key question. Answer in full.	
Purchasing business	22	49	Key question. Answer in full.	
Dividends or salary	22	50	Key question. Answer in full.	
Incorporation	22	46, 51	Key questions. Answer in full.	

BUSINESS TAX: THE 2005 EXAMS

The examination is a **three hour paper** divided into **two sections**.

FORMAT OF THE 2005 EXAMS

	Marks
Section A: 2 compulsory questions	55
Section B: 3 (out of 5) optional 15 mark questions	45
	100

Time allowed: 3 hours

Tax rates, allowances and benefits will be given in the examination paper.

Only core topics will be examined in Section A. A non-core topic may form part of a question (such as a chargeable gain in a corporation tax computation), but this will account for a maximum of ten marks. At least 40 of the 55 available marks in Section A will be of a computational nature.

- Question 1 will be on a corporate business (for approximately 30 marks).

- Question 2 will be on an unincorporated business and/or employees (for approximately 25 marks).

Question 1 might include some aspect of groups of companies if this topic is not examined in the optional section. However, any area examined will be very straightforward, and will be part of the non core topic marks. Prior to June 2005, the only aspect of groups of companies examinable in the compulsory section was that the number of associated companies might be given.

The questions in Section B will be a mix of computational and written, and include the minimisation or deferment of tax liability by the identification and application of relevant exemptions and reliefs.

- Question 3 will be on VAT (either for an incorporated business or an unincorporated business).

- Question 4 will be on capital gains (either for an incorporated business or an unincorporated business).

- Questions 5, 6 and 7 will be on any area of the syllabus.

If not examined as a distinct question, tax planning could form part of a question in either the compulsory or optional sections of the paper.

Analysis of past papers

> Note that past exam papers can be downloaded from the ACCA's website at www.accaglobal.com/students. However, please note that the exams on the website will not have been updated for Finance Act 2004.

December 2004 exam

Section A

1   CT computation for large company with profit adjustment and capital allowance/ IBAs calculation. Payment of CT

2   Partnership adjustment of profit, capital allowance calculation and allocation of profit. Calculation of IT and CGT for each partner.

Section B

3   Registration for VAT. Impact of VAT and effect of flat rate scheme.

4   Calculation of tax on gains for company disposing of building (with rollover relief) and shares. Impact of depreciating asset purchase on rollover relief.

5   UK company with overseas subsidiaries. Calculation of CT with DTR. Transfer pricing.

6   IT and NIC calculation and advice for employee considering two employment packages.

7   Calculation of income and gains for several years for sole trader making trading loss.

June 2004 exam

Section A

1   Computation of corporation tax liability in short accounting period. Due date for submission of CT return/correction of errors on return.

2   Adjustment of profit. Calculation of income tax and CGT payable. Due dates for payment of tax.

Section B

3   VAT tax point. Invoices. Calculation VAT payable

4   Chargeable gains: rollover relief. Incorporation. Gift relief

5   CT: Group relief

6   Employment v Self employment

7   Personal pension schemes

Examiner's comments

The performance at this diet was very good, and in complete contrast to the previous diet. The only question that caused any problems was question 7 on personal pensions. However the majority of candidates avoided this question.

December 2003 exam

Section A

1   Calculation of company's trading loss. Use of loss relief

2   P11D employees. Benefits for employees. Collection of tax on benefits.

Section B

3   VAT registration. Input tax recovery. Control visits by Customs

4   CGT for individual on shares. CT for company on disposal of warehouse

5   Overseas operations and effect on CT liability of UK company

6   Tax planning: choice of business medium

7   Change of accounting date

Examiner's comments

Performance at this diet was disappointing. This was largely due to poor answers to Question 2 and then attempting Question 3 when they might have been better advised to attempt one of the other optional questions instead. Despite my warning in my previous report for the June 2003 diet, it was apparent that too many candidates are not covering the whole syllabus when studying for this paper.

June 2003 exam

Section A

1   Long period of account for corporation tax. Rental income, admin and capital gains tax
2   Income tax liability of an employee compared to income tax liability for a self employed person

Section B

3   VAT: annual accounting/flat rate/cash accounting schemes
4   Capital gains: Shares, bonus issue, rights issue and takeover
5   Group relief and explanations
6   Tax planning: sale of a business
7   Badges of trade. Tax liability if (i) trade or (ii) capital gain

---

Examiner's comments

Although not quite up to the standard of the previous three diets, this was another very satisfactory performance. One of the reasons for the fall in standards seems to have been that Question 7 was set on a less predictable area of the syllabus than in the previous three diets. Quite a number of candidates did quite well on the compulsory section of the paper, but then struggled with the optional questions. In previous diets, the predictable nature of Question 7 (self-assessment, partnerships and trading losses have all been examined) has allowed these candidates to go on and achieve a pass mark. However, at this diet, Question 7 was answered quite badly, with the result that even some candidates who achieved 35 to 40 marks in the compulsory section failed to reach an overall pass mark. This should serve as a warning to not try and question spot, but for candidates to instead cover the whole syllabus when studying for this paper.

December 2002 exam

Section A

1   Adjustment of Schedule D Case I profits. Corporation tax computations. Corporation tax self assessment
2   Computation of assessable Schedule DII profits. Income tax computation. Keeping records

Section B

3   VAT: Registration, errors, deregistration
4   Computation of chargeable gains and capital gains tax liability
5   Capital gains groups
6   Employed/self employment
7   Corporation tax losses

Examiner's comments

Most candidates were very well prepared for the examination, and had obviously read the article concerning Paper 2.3, published in the Student Accountant. Of the seven questions on the paper it was again only question four on capital gains that was badly answered.

June 2002 exam

Section A

1   Corporation tax losses
2   Calculation of Schedule D Case I adjusted profit, income tax and Class 4 NICs

Section B

3   VAT: Calculation, penalties and cash accounting scheme
4   Capital gains: reliefs
5   Overseas aspects of corporation tax
6   Alternative employments contracts
7   Partnerships

Examiner's comments

It was an excellent performance at this diet, as evidenced by the high pass rate. It was apparent candidates were very well prepared, and had obviously read the examiner's articles published in Student Accountant. Of the seven questions on the paper, only question four on capital gains was badly answered.

December 2001 exam

Section A

1   CT61. Calculation of adjusted schedule D Case I profit. Computation corporation tax.
2   Income tax losses

Section B

3   VAT: registration, pre registration input VAT, invoices, tax points
4   Capital gains: rollover relief
5   Groups of companies
6   Trading as a sole trader followed by incorporation
7   Income tax self assessment

Examiner's comments

It was pleasing to see a very good performance at this first diet of the new syllabus, and it was apparent that many candidates were very well prepared. Most candidates had obviously read my articles in Student Accountant. However, a number of candidates would have benefited by taking a bit more time reading the questions and requirements.

Pilot Paper

Section A

1   Calculation of CT payable. Quarterly payments of CT
2   IT for employee/sole trader. Payment of IT

Section B

3   VAT registration. Input tax. Deregistrations
4   Business asset taper relief. Gains on shares
5   Group relief. CT liability
6   Employee/self employed distinction. NICs. IT under Sch D II or Sch E
7   Partnership profit allocation. Losses

Examiner's guidance

Relief for research and development expenditure

This is not examinable.

Income tax and Form CT61

The quarterly basis by which income tax is accounted for using Form CT61 is not examinable.

You should assume that any figures for patent royalties paid/received by a company are gross.

Double tax relief

The following are not examinable:

(a)   The restriction on the set off of underlying tax relief

(b)   The carry back/forward of unrelieved foreign tax.

Child tax credit

This is not examinable.

Averaging of profits for authors and creative artists

This is not examinable.

100% FYAs for low emission cars

In examination questions you should only treat cars as low emission if they are specifically described as such. You are not expected to know the 120g/km limit.

Quarterly instalment payments

Any question involving quarterly instalment payments will be based on a large company paying 100% of its corporation tax liability by instalments.

VAT flat rate scheme

The percentage needed for this purpose will be given to you in the examination.

Substantial shareholdings

The chargeable gains exemption for substantial shareholdings is not examinable.

100% FYA for water technologies

These are not examinable.

EXAM TECHNIQUE

Passing professional examinations is half about having the knowledge, and half about doing yourself full justice in the examination. You must have the right approach at the following times.

> **Before the exam**
> **Your time in the exam hall**

Before the exam

1   Set at least one **alarm** (or get an alarm call) for a morning exam.

2   Have **something to eat** but beware of eating too much; you may feel sleepy if your system is digesting a large meal.

3   Allow plenty of **time to get to the exam hall**; have your route worked out in advance and listen to news bulletins to check for potential travel problems.

4   **Don't forget** pens, pencils, rulers, erasers, watch. Also make sure you remember **entrance documentation** and **evidence of identity**.

5   Put **new batteries** into your calculator and take a spare set (or a spare calculator).

6   **Avoid discussion** about the exam with other candidates outside the exam hall.

Your time in the exam hall

1   *Read the instructions (the 'rubric') on the front of the exam paper carefully*

Check that the exam format hasn't changed. Examiners' reports often remark on the number of students who attempt too few - or too many - questions, or who attempt the wrong number of questions from different parts of the paper.

2   *Select questions carefully*

Read through the paper once, underlining the key words in the question and jotting down the most important points.   Select the optional questions that you feel you can answer best. You should base your selection on:

- The **topics** covered
- The **requirements of the whole question**
- How easy it will be to **apply the requirements** to the details you are given
- The availability of **easy marks**

Make sure that you are planning to answer the **right number of questions,** all the compulsory questions plus the correct number of optional questions.

3   *Plan your attack carefully*

Consider the **order** in which you are going to tackle questions. It is a good idea to start with your best question to boost your morale and get some easy marks 'in the bag'.

4   *Check the time allocation for each question*

Each mark carries with it a **time allocation** of 1.8 minutes (including time for selecting and reading questions, and checking answers). A 25 mark question therefore should be selected, completed and checked in 45 minutes. When time is up, you **must** go on to the next question or part. Going even one minute over the time allowed brings you a lot closer to failure.

5   *Read the question carefully and plan your answer*

Read through the question again very carefully when you come to answer it. Plan your answer taking into account how the answer should be **structured**, what the **format** should be and **how long** it should take.

Confirm before you start writing that your plan makes **sense**, covers **all relevant points** and does not include **irrelevant material.** Two minutes of planning plus eight minutes of writing is virtually certain to earn you more marks than ten minutes of writing.

6   *Answer the question set*

Particularly with written answers, make sure you **answer the question set**, and not the question you would have preferred to have been set.

7   *Gain the easy marks*

Include the obvious if it answers the question and don't try to produce the perfect answer.

Don't get bogged down in small parts of questions. If you find a part of a question difficult, get on with the rest of the question. If you are having problems with something, the chances are that everyone else is too.

8   *Produce an answer in the correct format*

The examiner will **state in the requirements** the format in which the question should be answered, for example in a report or memorandum.

9   *Follow the examiner's instructions*

You will **annoy** the examiner if you ignore him or her.

10   *Lay out your numerical computations and use workings correctly*

Make sure the layout fits the **type of question** and is in a style the examiner likes. Show all your **workings** clearly and explain what they mean. **Cross reference** them to your solution. This will help the examiner to follow your method (this is of particular importance where there may be several possible answers).

11   *Present a tidy paper*

You are a professional, and it should show in the **presentation of your work.** Students are penalised for poor presentation and so you should make sure that you write legibly, label diagrams clearly and lay out your work neatly. Markers of scripts each have hundreds of papers to mark; a badly written scrawl is unlikely to receive the same attention as a neat and well laid out paper.

12   *Stay until the end of the exam*

Use any spare time **checking and rechecking** your script. This includes checking:

- You have **filled out** the **candidate details correctly.**
- Question parts and workings are **labelled clearly.**
- Aids to navigation such as **headers and underlining** are used effectively.
- **Spelling, grammar** and **arithmetic** are correct.

13   *Don't discuss an exam with other candidates afterwards*

There's nothing more you can do about it so why discuss it?

14 *Don't worry if you feel you have performed badly in the exam*

It is more than likely that the other candidates will have found the exam difficult too. Don't forget that there is a competitive element in these exams. As soon as you get up to leave the exam hall, *forget* **that exam** and think about the next - or, if it is the last one, celebrate!

> BPP's *Learning to Learn Accountancy* book gives further invaluable advice on how to approach the day of the exam.

USEFUL ARTICLES AND USEFUL WEBSITES

The websites below provide additional sources of information of relevance to your studies for *Business Taxation.*

- ACCA   www.accaglobal.com

- BPP   www.bpp.com

In particular, you should regularly check the ACCA's website to see if any articles relevant to Paper 2.3 have been published. It is essential that you read any such articles. A particularly important article is the Finance Act 2004 article. The Paper 2.3 section of this article was written by your examiner and you should ensure you read it. It is available on the ACCA website or in the November/December edition of Student Accountant.

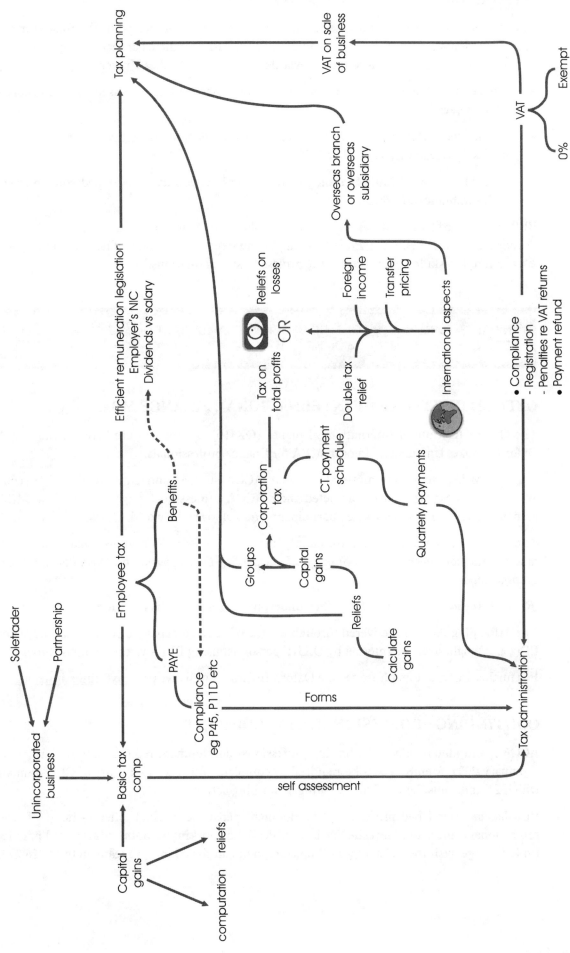

BPP
PROFESSIONAL EDUCATION

OXFORD BROOKES BSc IN APPLIED ACCOUNTING

The standard required of candidates completing Part 2 is that required in the final year of a UK degree. Students completing Parts 1 and 2 will have satisfied the examination requirement for an honours degree in Applied Accounting, awarded by Oxford Brookes University.

To achieve the degree, you must also submit two pieces of work based on a **Research and Analysis Project.**

- A 5,000 word **Report** on your chosen topic, which demonstrates that you have acquired the necessary research, analytical and IT skills.

- A 1,500 word **Key Skills Statement**, indicating how you have developed your interpersonal and communication skills.

BPP was selected by the ACCA and Oxford Brookes University to produce the official text *Success in your Research and Analysis Project* to support students in this task. The book pays particular attention to key skills not covered in the professional examinations.

> AN ORDER FORM FOR THE OXFORD BROOKES PROJECT TEXT CAN BE FOUND AT THE END OF THIS PRACTICE AND REVISION KIT.

OXFORD INSTITUTE OF INTERNATIONAL FINANCE MBA

The Oxford Institute of International Finance (OXIIF), a joint venture between the ACCA and Oxford Brookes University, offers an MBA for finance professionals.

For this MBA, credits are awarded for your ACCA studies, and entry to the MBA course is available to those who have completed their ACCA professional stage studies. The MBA was launched in 2002 and has attracted participants from all over the world.

The qualification features an introductory module (*Markets, Management and Strategy*). Other modules include *Global Business Strategy, Managing Self Development,* and *Organisational Change & Transformation.*

Research Methods are also taught, as they underpin the **research dissertation.**

The MBA programme is delivered through the use of targeted paper study materials, developed by BPP, and taught over the Internet by OXIIF personnel using BPP's virtual campus software.

For further information, please see the Oxford Institute's website: www.oxfordinstitute.org

CONTINUING PROFESSIONAL DEVELOPMENT

ACCA is introducing a new continuing professional development requirement for members from 1 January 2005. Members will be required to complete and record 40 units of CPD annually, of which 21 units must be verifiable learning or training activity.

BPP has an established professional development department which offers a range of relevant, professional courses to reflect the needs of professional working in both industry and practice. To find out more, visit the website: www.bpp.com/pd or call the client care team on 0845 226 2422

Questions

> **CORPORATE BUSINESSES**
>
> Questions 1 to 25 cover corporate businesses, the subject of Part A of the BPP Study Text for Paper 2.3.

1 PREPARATION QUESTION: SUNDRY ADJUSTMENTS

Advise the management of a limited company as to the consequences for corporation tax purposes of the following transactions which have occurred during its last accounting period.

(a) Loan interest of £5,000 was received. The borrower (a UK company) advised that no tax had been deducted from the interest. The loan was a non-trading investment.

(b) £100,000 was received from the sale of a factory in respect of which capital allowances had been claimed. The factory was purchased new and first used in 1988. It had always been used as a factory.

(c) Defalcations of cash by staff have been discovered in the sum of £8,000, of which £5,000 was attributable to junior staff and the balance to a member of the board of directors.

(d) Additional retail premises were acquired for £40,000, which was well below normal market value due to the dilapidated state of these premises. Repairs and renewals expenditure of £60,000 had to be incurred.

(e) Expenditure totalling £128,000 was incurred in entertaining the company's own staff, customers' staff and representatives from business agencies.

Guidance notes

1 You can deal with each item separately, not worrying about the other items. The important thing is to state the treatment of each item clearly.

2 Capital allowances are not the only tax aspect of the sale of the factory to consider.

3 With the defalcations, the position of the guilty party is relevant. Directors run the business, and are therefore treated differently from junior staff.

4 With the retail premises, there is a legal case of particular relevance.

5 When entertaining expenditure is incurred, the tax treatment depends on who was entertained.

2 PREPARATION QUESTION: CAPITAL AND REVENUE

In taxation, the distinction between capital and revenue expenditure is crucial.

Required

Indicate how this distinction is applied when dealing with items appearing in a company's profit and loss account, supporting your answer by reference to relevant case law.

Guidance notes

1 Start by outlining the distinction. Why does it matter if expenditure is capital or if a profit is a capital gain?

2 Then explain what expenditure is likely to be treated as capital, giving some examples. A good area is repairs and improvements.

3 Cite cases by name if you can, but always make sure you outline the facts and show clearly why the case is relevant.

4 Finally, consider what makes a profit a capital gain.

3   TRUNK LTD   *27 mins*

The profit and loss account of Trunk Ltd, a manufacturing company, for the year ended 31 March 2005 showed a loss of £42,000 after accounting for the under-noted items.

Note	Expenditure	£	£	Income	£
(1)	Premium on lease		2,000		
	Depreciation		9,500	Discount received	3,200
	Patent fees (not royalties)		4,000	Insurance recovery re flood	
	Debenture interest (gross:			damage to stock	6,500
	trading relationship)		8,000	Rents received	10,000
	Loss on sale of lorry		6,000	Gain on sale of plant	7,400
	Bad debts:				
	Amounts written off	4,000			
	Increase special provision	2,000			
		6,000			
	Less:				
	Reduction general provision	1,000			
			5,000		
(2)	Entertainment expenses		2,600		
	Legal fees:				
	Re new lease		3,200		
	Re recovery of loan to former employee		1,200		
	Re employees' service contracts		600		
(3)	General expenses		4,000		
(4)	Repairs and renewals		6,400		

Capital allowances for the accounting period were agreed at £7,160.

Notes

(1) This represents the amount written off in respect of a premium of £20,000 paid by the company on being granted a ten-year lease on its premises on 1 April 2004.

(2) Entertainment consists of expenditure on:

	£
Entertaining customers	1,200
Staff dance (40 people)	800
Gifts to customers of food hampers	600

(3) General expenses comprise:

	£
Penalty for late VAT return	2,200
Parking fines on company cars	300
Fees for employees attending courses	1,500

(4) Included in this figure for repairs is an amount of £5,000 incurred in installing new windows in a recently-acquired second-hand warehouse. This building had suffered fire damage resulting in all of its windows being blown out shortly before being acquired by Trunk Ltd. Other repairs were of a routine nature.

Required

Compute the adjusted Schedule D Case I figure for the above period.

Your answer should show clearly your reasons for your treatment of each of the above items including those items not included in your computation.   **(15 marks)**

4   SCHEDULE D ADJUSTMENTS

27 mins

An examination of the draft accounts of your company for the year ended 31 March 2005 reveals the following details in respect of specific items of expenditure and income. The draft accounts showed a profit of £290,000.

EXPENDITURE

(a) Throughout the year, two of the directors were seconded to work elsewhere. One worked for Oxfam - a leading charity - and his salary, paid by your company, was £22,000. The other worked for a subsidiary company in the group and his salary, also paid by your company, was £24,000.

(b) Damages of £30,000 were paid to a customer who was injured by a falling crate while visiting your factory. Only £18,000 was recovered from your public liability insurers.

(c) During the year the company purchased freehold offices for £40,000. Your chief engineer estimated that it would cost £2,000 to get them ready for use. In the event it cost £12,000. The amount spent purchasing the offices was capitalised but the repair expenditure of £12,000 was deducted in the profit and loss account.

(d) Bad debts were written off amounting to £6,000. The appropriate ledger account for the year showed:

	£		£
Trade debts written off	8,000	Balances b/fwd:	
Employee loans written off	2,000	Special provision	10,000
Balances c/fwd:		General provisions	8,000
Special provision	12,000	Bad debts recovered	3,000
General provision	5,000	Profit and loss account	6,000
	27,000		27,000

(e) Because of an overall contraction in trade, a supervisor was made redundant and given a severance payment of £18,000. His statutory redundancy entitlement was £11,000.

INCOME

(f) During the year the company obtained recoveries from its insurers amounting to £32,000. These related to damage caused and repairs completed in the year to 31 March 2004 and comprised:

	£
In respect of repairs to the general office	18,000
In respect of repairs to property let by the company to another firm	14,000
	32,000

(g) Goods were sold to a subsidiary in the Caribbean for £80,000. Had they been sold to a UK customer the price would have been £120,000.

Required

Compute the adjusted Schedule D Case I profit starting with the profit of £290,000 shown by the accounts. Give reasons for your adjustments, quoting case law where appropriate.

(15 marks)

5 PREPARATION QUESTION: CORPORATION TAX COMPUTATION

Abel Ltd, a UK trading company, produced the following results for the year ended 31 March 2005.

	£
Income	
Adjusted trading profit	45,000
Rental income	15,000
Bank deposit interest accrued (non-trading investment)	4,000
Capital gains: 25 September 2004	35,000
28 March 2005	7,000
(There were capital losses of £40,000 brought forward at 1 April 2004.)	
Trading losses brought forward at 1 April 2004	20,000
Charges paid	
Gift aid donation	7,000

Required

(a) Compute the mainstream corporation tax (MCT) payable by Abel Ltd for the above accounting period.

(b) Advise the directors of the effect on the company's tax liability of their decision to pay a dividend to a non-corporate shareholder on 5 June 2004 of £20,000.

Guidance notes

1   In working out a company's profits chargeable to corporation tax (PCTCT), we must bring together all taxable profits, including gains. You must therefore start by drawing up a working, and picking out from the question all relevant profit figures.

2   Once you have found the PCTCT, you can consider the rate of tax. You should find that small companies marginal relief applies. If you do not, look carefully to see whether you have missed anything.

3   Having completed your computation, you should move on to part (b). As the amount of the proposed dividend is given you are required to calculate any additional tax liability.

6 PREPARATION QUESTION: SMALL COMPANIES TAXATION

Robo Ltd started trading on July 2004 and made up its first accounts to 31 March 2005.

The sole shareholder and director of Robo Ltd is Robert Armitage.

In the period between 1 July 2004 and 31 March 2005, the following income was received and expenses incurred.

	£
Trading profits	50,000
Bank interest received	313
Gift aid donation paid	500
Dividend paid to Robert	10,000
Van bought	10,000
Computer	2,000
Car (low emission) (20% private use by Robert)	15,000
Car (normal emission) (15% private use by salesman)	7,000

Required

Compute the corporation tax payable by Robo Ltd for the period ending 31 March 2005.

6

Guidance notes

1   A good place to start would be to work out the capital allowances computation.

2   Then you can work out the PCTCT

3   What is the effect of a short accounting period on the limits for marginal rate relief?

4   How does the payment of the dividend to Robert affect the corporation tax computation?

7   PREPARATION QUESTION: LONG PERIOD OF ACCOUNT

Hartlington Ltd is a UK resident company. It was incorporated in 1998 and began its trade of manufacturing paper-making machinery in the same year. The company's recent results are as follows.

	Year ended 31 March 2003 £	Period 1 April 2003 to 30 Sept 2004 £
Trading profits (as adjusted for taxation but before capital allowances)	148,000	477,900
Bank interest accrued (non-trading investment)	18,000	20,500
Chargeable gains on sales of shares	108,000	176,250
Dividends received (net) from UK companies	788	9,205
Gift aid donations paid	3,750	5,250

Other relevant information is as follows.

(a)   *Plant and machinery*

The balance in the pool at 1 April 2002 was £213,000. Purchases and sales of assets qualifying for capital allowances were as follows.

Year ended 31 March 2003

Purchases
31.1.03   Six cars for sales staff at a cost of £6,000 each
31.3.03   Car for the managing director £16,500

Period 1 April 2003 to 30 September 2004

Purchases
6.5.03   Plant and machinery £119,583
30.9.03   Car for the chief accountant £7,800
7.6.04   New computer equipment £23,000

Sales
30.11.03   Plant and machinery £70,000 (cost £150,000 in 1998)
1.6.04   Two cars at a price of £1,997 each (both were purchased in 2000 for £4,500 each)

None of the expenditure is to be treated as incurred on either short-life assets or on long-life assets. None of the cars are low emission cars. The business is a small enterprise for FYA purposes.

(b) Payments and receipts in the period from 1 April 2003 to 30 September 2004 were as follows.

(i) Bank interest received £
30.9.03 5,250
31.3.04 9,791
30.9.04 5,459

All interest was received at the end of the six month period for which it accrued.

(ii) Chargeable gains
30.6.04 176,250

(iii) Dividends received (net)
30.9.03 1,000
31.3.04 598
30.9.04 7,785

(iv) Gift aid donations paid
30.6.03 3,750
30.6.04 1,500

Required

Calculate the corporation tax payable for the periods in the question and state the due dates of payment.

Guidance notes

1 You are asked to calculate the corporation tax payable for three accounting periods. The simplest (and quickest) way to do this is to set up three columns.

2 Set out the computation in the normal way, beginning with trading profits, followed by capital allowances, investment income, gains and charges.

3 The resulting figure is profits chargeable to corporation tax (PCTCT). Remember that dividends plus tax credits are added to PCTCT to calculate 'profits'. Dividends are grossed up by multiplying by $^{100}/_{90}$.

4 Calculating the tax payable involves a number of steps, which should be taken in the right order.

(a) Decide which financial year(s) the accounting period falls into, so that the appropriate tax rates and upper and lower limits are used.

(b) Calculate the corporation tax.

(c) If relevant, calculate and deduct marginal relief, remembering to adjust the limits for periods of less than 12 months.

5 Don't overlook the easy mark available for stating the due date for payment of the tax in each period.

8 **UNFORESEEN ULTRASONICS LIMITED** *47 mins*

Unforeseen Ultrasonics Limited (UUL) is a United Kingdom resident company which manufactures accessories for telecommunication systems. It has no associated companies.

The company's results for the year ended 31 December 2004 were as follows.

	£
Trading profits (adjusted for taxation but before capital allowances) (note 1)	2,300,000
Bank interest receivable (non-trading investment)	1,500
Debenture interest received (non-trading investment) (note 4)	80,000
Payment under the gift aid scheme to a national charity (paid September 2004)	5,000

The company has traded in a purpose built unit since 1 January 1999. The total cost of the unit was made up as follows:

	£
Freehold land	50,000
Manufacturing area	240,000
Canteen	30,000
Design office	90,000
General office	70,000
	480,000

On 1 July 2004 an extension to the general office was completed costing £60,000.

On 1 January 2004 the tax written-down values of plant and machinery were as follows.

	£
Pool	190,000
Short-life asset	4,000

The short-life asset was purchased on 1 December 1999 and was sold on 31 July 2004 for £10,000.

On 1 August 2004 a new car (not low emission) costing £18,000 was purchased for the managing director. The car previously used by him had cost £10,000 in April 2002 and was sold for £8,000. A new precision engineering machine was purchased on 1 August 2004 for £56,250.

On 1 September 2004, Unforeseen Ultrasonics Limited sold a piece of land for £72,493. The land had been acquired as an investment in July 1990 for £27,000.

Notes

1   In arriving at the adjusted trading profit an adjustment had been made for small capital additions totalling £24,375 which the company had written off as repairs but which the Inspector of Taxes had insisted were added back.

2   On 1 January 2004 the company had capital losses brought forward of £30,000.

3   On 1 January 2004 the company had trading losses brought forward of £600,000.

4   The debenture was invested in on 1 April 2004. All amounts accrued in the nine months to 31 December 2004 were received in the period.

5   The company paid corporation tax at the full rate in its accounting period ended 31 December 2003.

6   The company is a small enterprise for capital allowance purposes.

Required

Calculate the mainstream corporation tax payable for the year ended 31 December 2004 and state the due date(s) for payment of this amount and the amount of any losses carried forward. **(26 marks)**

Assume indexation factor July 1990 – September 2004 0.603

9   PLUG-IN LTD   *54 mins*

Plug-In Ltd is a UK resident company that manufactures computer peripherals. The company's summarised profit and loss account for the year ended 31 December 2004 is as follows:

	£	£
Gross profit		2,404,890
Operating expenses		
Bad debts (note 1)	18,950	
Depreciation	93,770	
Gifts and donations (note 2)	4,250	
Patent royalties (note 3)	14,800	
Professional fees (note 4)	20,040	
Rent and rates (note 5)	112,000	
Other expenses (note 6)	148,790	
		(412,600)
Operating profit		1,992,290
Income from investments		
Bank interest (note 7)		16,600
		2,008,890
Interest payable (note 8)		(120,000)
Profit before taxation		1,888,890

Note 1 – Bad debts

Bad debts are as follows:

	£
Trade debts recovered from previous years	(1,350)
Decrease in specific bad debt provision	(2,700)
Increase in general provision for doubtful debts	23,000
	18,950

Note 2 – Gifts and donations

Gifts and donations are as follows:

	£
Gifts to customers (diaries costing £30 each and displaying Plug-In Ltd's name)	2,400
Gifts to customers (hampers of food costing £100 each)	1,100
Donation to national charity (made under the Gift Aid scheme)	750
	4,250

Note 3 – Patent royalties

Patent royalties of £11,200 were paid on 31 October 2004, and £3,600 was accrued at 31 December 2004. There was no accrual at 31 December 2003. The figures for patent royalties are all gross. The patent relates to the company's trade.

Note 4 – Professional fees

Professional fees are as follows:

	£
Accountancy and audit fee	8,040
Legal fees in connection with the issue of share capital	10,600
The cost of registering the company's trademark	1,400
	20,040

Note 5 – Rent and rates

Rent and rates includes a premium of £60,000 that was paid on 1 January 2004 for the grant of a 15-year lease on an office building.

Note 6 – Other expenses

Other expenses include £6,740 for entertaining customers, £4,780 for entertaining employees, and the cost for seconding an employee to a charity of £3,600. The remaining expenses are all allowable.

Note 7 – Bank interest

The bank interest was received on 31 December 2004. The bank deposits are held for non-trading purposes.

Note 8 – Interest payable

The interest is in respect of a debenture loan that has been used for trading purposes. Interest of £60,000 was paid on 30 June 2004 and again on 31 December 2004.

Note 9 – Industrial building

On 1 April 2004 Plug-In Ltd purchased a second-hand factory for £440,000 (including £130,000 for land and £95,000 for general offices). The factory was originally constructed at a cost of £486,500 (including £145,000 for land and £105,000 for general offices), and was brought into use on 1 October 2000. The factory has always been used for industrial purposes.

Note 10 – Plant and machinery

On 1 January 2004 the tax written down values of plant and machinery were as follows:

	£
General pool	124,400
Short-life asset	11,200

The following transactions took place during the year ended 31 December 2004:

		Cost/(Proceeds)
		£
5 March	Purchased equipment	84,000
22 June	Purchased a computer	9,800
11 September	Purchased a motor car	10,200
15 October	Sold a lorry	(11,800)
12 December	Sold the short-life asset	(4,600)

The lorry sold on 15 October 2004 for £11,800 originally cost £18,000. Plug-In Ltd is a medium-sized company for capital allowance purposes.

Note 11 – Other information

Plug-In Ltd has no associated companies. For the year ended 31 December 2003 Plug-In Ltd had profits chargeable to corporation tax of £1,800,000.

Required

(a) Calculate Plug-In Ltd's tax adjusted Schedule DI profit for the year ended 31 December 2004.   (22 marks)

(b) Calculate Plug-In Ltd's corporation tax liability for the year ended 31 December 2004.
                                                                        (4 marks)

(c) (i) Explain why Plug-In Ltd would have been required to make quarterly instalment payments in respect of its corporation tax liability for the year ended 31 December 2004.   (2 marks)

    (ii) Explain how and when Plug-In Ltd's corporation tax liability for the year ended 31 December 2004 will have been paid. You should assume that the company's profits accrued evenly throughout the year.   (2 marks)

                                                                     (30 marks)

10   PREPARATION QUESTION: PLANT AND A FACTORY

Freddie Ltd prepared accounts for the ten month period to 31 March 2005. The company is a small company for the purposes of calculating capital allowances.

The following capital expenditure was incurred in this trading period.

(i)	30 January 2005	New computer equipment costing £2,500.
(ii)	1 February 2005	New motor car costing £16,000, secondhand motor car costing £5,000. Neither car was a low emission car.
(iii)	2 March 2005	New plant costing £32,400, secondhand plant costing £33,442, secondhand factory and land costing £50,000 (including land £15,000) which had been purchased new by the original owner on 5 June 1990 for £10,000 (including land £2,500), and had always been used as a factory.
(iv)	31 March 2005	Extension to the factory built for £222,000.

Prior to 1 June 2004, all equipment was leased so there were no tax written down values brought forward on this date.

Freddie Ltd's business qualifies as a small enterprise for capital allowance purposes.

Required

(a) Calculate the maximum capital allowances which can be claimed by Freddie Ltd in this accounting period.

(b) Set out the amount of tax benefit the reliefs calculated in (a) would yield and when this benefit would be obtained.

(c) Outline the relief available to Freddie Ltd in respect of expenditure on office accommodation.

Assume tax rates and allowances for FY 2004 throughout this period.

Guidance notes

1   You should first read through the question, and note all the different types of asset involved.

2   You can then plan how your answer will look. Because there is only one accounting period, there is no real need for a multi-column computation.

3   Each type of asset should then be tackled separately. By breaking the question down into small pieces in this way, it becomes much more manageable.

4   Note the length of the accounting period. Will this affect WDAs or FYAs?

11   UNFORGETTABLE UNITS LIMITED

50 mins

Unforgettable Units Limited (UUL) is a United Kingdom resident company which manufactures self-assemble furniture. It has no associated companies and has always made accounts up to 31 August. In the year ended 31 August 2004 the company's profit was £822,875 which was arrived at *after* charging and crediting the following items.

Expenditure		£
Gift aid donations paid		58,000
Legal expenses	(note 2)	10,000
Bad debts	(note 3)	42,000
Income		
Debenture interest	(note 4)	64,000
Bank interest	(note 5)	5,000
Dividend	(note 6)	11,250

Note 1

Unforgettable Units Limited is a medium-sized company with a turnover in the year ended 31 August 2004 of £4,000,000. The average number of employees during the accounting period was 160.

Note 2

Legal expenses incurred were:

Fine for not fitting saws with protective guards	£10,000

Note 3

Bad debts account

	£		£
Trading debts written off in year	23,000	Balances at 1.9.03	
		– Specific	57,000
Balances at 31.8.04		– General	40,000
– Specific	92,000	Recovery of bad debt previously	
– General	35,000	written off	11,000
		Profit and loss account	42,000
	150,000		150,000

Note 4

Debenture interest receivable

	£		£
1.9.03 b/f	–	30.4.04 received	61,000
Profit and loss account	64,000	31.8.04 c/f	3,000
	64,000		64,000

The interest was non-trading income.

Note 5

Bank interest

The £5,000 was credited to the company's bank account on 31 July 2004. The interest is non-trading interest.

Note 6

On 1 December 2003 Unforgettable Units Limited received a dividend from another UK company of £11,250. This amount represents the actual amount received without any adjustment for tax credits.

Note 7

Plant and machinery

On 1 September 2003 the tax written down values of plant and machinery was:

	£
Main pool	100,000

New machinery, which is not to be treated either a 'short-life' asset or a 'long-life' asset, costing £35,000 was purchased on 31 January 2004. On 1 May 2004 a car that had cost £7,500 in 2001 was sold for £2,000 and replaced with one costing £13,000 (not a low emission car).

Note 8

Industrial buildings allowance

On 1 January 2004 Unforgettable Units Limited purchased a factory for £150,000 from Cape Capsules Limited whose accounting date was 31 March. The factory was built for Cape Capsules Limited at a cost of £250,000 and had been brought into use on 1 August 1998. Maximum industrial buildings allowances had been claimed by Cape Capsules Limited. The factory has not been used for non-trading purposes.

Required

Calculate the corporation tax payable by Unforgettable Units Limited for the year ended 31 August 2004. You should give reasons for your treatment of the legal expenses in Note 3.

(28 marks)

12   PREPARATION QUESTION: CARRYING BACK A LOSS

Galbraith Ltd is a company resident in the United Kingdom making garments for sale to the tourist industry at its factory in Callander. It started to trade on 1 April 2002. The company's results for the first three years are as follows.

	Year ended 31 March		
	2003	*2004*	*2005*
	£	£	£
Trading profit/(loss) (as adjusted for taxation)	125,000	(465,000)	50,000
Bank interest accrued (non-trading investment)	263,000	10,000	24,000
Chargeable gains /(allowable loss)	60,360	(7,000)	3,000
Dividends received from UK companies (net) (January)	6,750	3,000	3,750
Gift aid donation	40,000	47,000	30,000

Required

(a) Calculate the corporation tax liabilities for the three years after claiming maximum loss relief at the earliest possible times. Comment on the effectiveness of the reliefs. Assume FY 2004 rates and allowances apply throughout.

(b) In respect of the mainstream corporation tax for the accounting period ended 31 March 2005, state when this will be due for payment and state the filing date.

Guidance notes

1   In requirement (a) you are alerted to the likelihood of encountering losses.

2   First, set out the figures for trading profits and leave space for losses carried forward under s 393(1) ICTA 1988.

3   Set out the remainder of the profits subject to tax and then deduct losses from the total. Questions usually require loss relief to be claimed as quickly as possible. Remember that s 393A(1) ICTA 1988 requires losses to be set off first against total profits of the loss-making accounting period. Only after these have been extinguished can losses be carried back. Any remaining losses are carried forward, but may only be set against trading profits (not total profits).

4   Remember that certain companies pay corporation tax at the starting rate of 0%. Does the starting rate of corporation tax apply in this case?

5   Remember that certain companies are required to pay for their anticipated corporation tax liability by quarterly instalments. Does this apply to Galbraith Ltd?

13   LOSER LTD   *27 mins*

Loser Ltd's results for the year ended 30 June 2002, the nine month period ended 31 March 2003, the year ended 31 March 2004 and the year ended 31 March 2005 are as follows:

	Year ended 30 June 2002	*Period ended 31 March 2003*	*Year ended 31 March 2004*	*Year ended 31 March 2005*
	£	£	£	£
Schedule DI profit/(loss)	98,400	(25,700)	43,700	(78,300)
Schedule A profit	(3,600)	4,500	8,100	5,600
Gift Aid paid (gross)	(1,400)	(800)	(1,200)	(1,100)

Required

(a)   State the factors that will influence a company's choice of loss relief claims. You are not expected to consider group relief.   (3 marks)

(b)   Assuming that Loser Ltd claims relief for its losses as early as possible, calculate the company's profits chargeable to corporation tax for the year ended 30 June 2002, the nine month period ended 31 March 2003, the year ended 31 March 2004 and the year ended 31 March 2005. Your answer should show the amount of unrelieved losses as at 31 March 2005.   (10 marks)

(c)   Explain how your answer to (b) would have differed if Loser Ltd had ceased trading on 31 March 2005.   (2 marks)

(15 marks)

14   PREPARATION QUESTION: A BUILDING AND SHARES

Jolly Cove Ltd, which commenced trading in 1983, makes up its accounts annually to 31 March, and has no associated companies.

During its accounting year ended 31 March 2005 Jolly Cove Ltd disposed of the following assets.

(a)   In June 2004, a non-industrial building was sold for £200,000. It had been purchased in July 1986 for £65,000.

(b)   In July 2004, 4,000 shares in Z plc were sold for £22,000. The shares in Z plc had been acquired as follows.

May 1983	2,000 shares for £4,000
March 1987	2,000 shares for £5,000

There were no capital losses brought forward.

Jolly Cove Ltd's taxable profits for the year ended 31 March 2005, excluding capital gains, were £2,000,000.

Required

(a) Calculate the amount of corporation tax payable as a result of the above transactions.

(b) Advise Jolly Cove Ltd as to the consequences of its replacing the building referred to above with another building costing either £225,000 or alternatively £175,000.

Assume indexation factors:

July 1986 – June 2004	0.893
May 1983 – April 1985	0.065
April 1985 – March 1987	0.061
March 1987 – July 2004	0.837

Guidance notes

1 The building requires a basic capital gains computation.

2 The shares are in the FA 1985 pool. The FA 1985 pool includes indexation within it, firstly up to its starting point April 1985 and then up to each purchase or sale. Strictly, there is no need to round indexation post April 1985, but for exam purposes you may use the rounded factors given to you in the exam.

3 Part (b) is about rollover relief. Remember that the general rule is that someone who sells an asset and claims rollover relief will still be taxed on the gain immediately, to the extent of the cash they put into their pocket instead of into the new asset.

15   ASTUTE LTD   *27 mins*

Astute Ltd sold a factory on 15 February 2005 for £320,000. The factory was purchased on 24 October 1998 for £164,000, and was extended at a cost of £37,000 during March 2000. During May 2001 the roof of the factory was replaced at a cost of £24,000 following a fire. Astute Ltd incurred legal fees of £3,600 in connection with the purchase of the factory, and legal fees of £6,200 in connection with the disposal.

Indexation factors are as follows:

October 1998 to February 2005	0.132
March 2000 to February 2005	0.106
May 2001 to February 2005	0.069

Astute Ltd is considering the following alternative ways of reinvesting the proceeds from the sale of its factory:

1 A freehold warehouse can be purchased for £340,000.

2 A freehold office building can be purchased for £275,000.

3 A leasehold factory on a 40-year lease can be acquired for a premium of £350,000.

The reinvestment will take place during May 2005. All of the above buildings have been, or will be, used for business purposes.

Required

(a) State the conditions that must be met in order that rollover relief can be claimed. You are not expected to list the categories of asset that qualify for rollover relief.   (3 marks)

(b) Before taking account of any available rollover relief, calculate Astute Ltd's chargeable gain in respect of the disposal of the factory.   (5 marks)

(c) Advise Astute Ltd of the rollover relief that will be available in respect of each of the three alternative reinvestments. Your answer should include details of the base cost of the replacement asset for each alternative.   (7 marks)

(15 marks)

16   EAGLE LTD   *54 mins*

Eagle Ltd is a UK resident company that manufactures aeroplane components. The company's results for the year ended 31 March 2005 are summarised as follows:

	£
Trading loss (as adjusted for taxation but before taking account of capital allowances and patent royalties)	(259,900)
Income from property (note 3)	55,900
Profit on disposal of shares (note 4)	43,200
Patent royalties payable (note 5)	(20,000)
Donation to charity (note 6)	(3,000)

Note 1 – Industrial building

Eagle Ltd had a new factory constructed at a cost of £350,000 that was brought into use on 1 July 2004. The cost is made up as follows:

	£
Land	87,500
Site preparation	12,000
Architect's fees	5,000
Canteen for employees	32,000
General offices	72,500
Factory	141,000
	350,000

Note 2 – Plant and machinery

On 1 April 2004 the tax written down values of plant and machinery were as follows:

	£
General pool	64,700
Expensive motor car	14,700

The expensive motor car was sold on 15 February 2005 for £12,400.

The following assets were purchased during the year ended 31 March 2005:

		£
20 October 2004	Lorry	22,400
18 March 2005	Motor car	11,300

Eagle Ltd is a small company for capital allowance purposes.

Note 3 – Income from property

Eagle Ltd lets out two warehouses that are surplus to requirements.

The first warehouse was empty from 1 April to 30 June 2004, but was let from 1 July 2004. On that date the company received a premium of £50,000 for the grant of an eight-year lease, and the annual rent of £12,600 which is payable in advance.

The second warehouse was let until 31 December 2004 at an annual rent of £8,400. On that date the tenant left owing three months rent which the company is not able to recover. The roof of the warehouse was repaired at a cost of £6,700 during February 2005.

Note 4 – Profit on disposal of shares

The profit on disposal of shares is in respect of a 2% shareholding in a public company that was sold on 22 December 2004 for £156,000. The shareholding was purchased on 5 June 1997 for £112,800. The indexation allowance from June 1997 to April 1998 is £3,610, and from June 1997 to December 2004 it is £20,268.

Note 5 – Patent royalties payable

The figure for patent royalties payable is calculated as follows:

	£
Payments made	20,600
Accrued at 31 March 2005	1,600
	22,200
Accrued at 1 April 2004	2,200
	20,000

The patent royalties are paid for the purposes of the company's trade.

Note 6 – Donation to charity

The donation to charity was made under the Gift Aid scheme.

Note 7 – Other information

Eagle Ltd has no associated companies. Its results for the year ended 30 September 2003 and for the six month period ended 31 March 2004 were as follows:

	Year ended 30 September 2003	Period ended 31 March 2004
	£	£
Schedule DI profit	152,100	65,700
Schedule A profit/(loss)	(4,600)	18,700
Capital gain/(loss)	(8,900)	18,200
Donation to charity (gross)	(2,300)	(2,600)

Required

(a) Calculate Eagle Ltd's Schedule DI trading loss for the year ended 31 March 2005. You should assume that the company claims the maximum available capital allowances.
(10 marks)

(b) Assuming that Eagle Ltd claims relief for its Schedule DI trading loss under s.393A ICTA 1988 against total profits, calculate the company's profits chargeable to corporation tax for the year ended 30 September 2003, the six month period ended 31 March 2004, and the year ended 31 March 2005. Your answer should show the amount of unrelieved trading losses as at 31 March 2005. (17 marks)

(c) Describe the alternative ways in which Eagle Ltd could have relieved its Schedule DI trading loss for the year ended 31 March 2005. (3 marks)

(30 marks)

17   PREPARATION QUESTION: FOREIGN TAX

Mumbo Ltd, a UK resident trading company, owns 6% of the share capital of Z Inc and 8% of the share capital of X SA. Neither of these companies is resident in the UK for tax purposes. In addition, Mumbo Ltd has a controlling interest in four UK resident companies.

The following information relates to Mumbo Ltd's 12 month accounting period ended 30 April 2005.

	£	£
Income		
Schedule D Case I trading profits		550,000
Schedule D Case V		
Dividend from Z Inc – after deduction of withholding tax of 28%	36,000	
Dividend from X SA – after deduction of withholding tax of 5%	38,000	
		74,000
Charge paid		
Gift aid donation		60,000

Required

Compute the MCT payable for the above period by Mumbo Ltd, showing clearly the relief for double taxation. Assume FY 2004 tax rates and allowances apply throughout.

Guidance notes

1   This question requires you to compute mainstream corporation tax on overseas income, taking account of double taxation relief.

2   Charges should be set first against UK profits and then against the overseas income which has borne the lowest rate of overseas tax.

3   The restriction of double taxation relief to the lower of the overseas tax and the UK tax on the overseas income must be applied to each source of income separately.

18   B AND W LTD   *27 mins*

B Ltd acquired 80% of the voting rights of W Ltd in December 2004. Both companies are resident in the United Kingdom. B Ltd has, for several years, owned 5% of the voting capital of P Inc, a company resident abroad.

The following information relates to B Ltd for its twelve-month accounting period ended 31 January 2005.

	£
INCOME	
Adjusted trading profits	296,000
Capital gains	30,000
Dividend from P Inc (net of 20% overseas tax)	1,600
Debenture interest received 30 November 2004 (non trading investment)	8,000
FII (inclusive of tax credit) received in May 2004	32,000
CHARGES PAID	
Gift Aid to charity	18,000

W Ltd also made up accounts for the twelve months to 31 January 2005 and its only taxable income consisted of trading profits of £6,000.

There were no accruals of debenture interest at the beginning or end of the year. The debenture interest was received gross from another UK company.

Required

Compute the mainstream corporation tax (MCT) payable by both B Ltd and W Ltd for the above accounting period, assuming all appropriate claims are made.

Show clearly your treatment of double tax relief.   **(15 marks)**

19   WASH PLC   *27 mins*

Wash plc is a UK resident company that manufactures kitchen equipment. The company's Schedule DI profit for the year ended 31 March 2005 is £1,600,000. Wash plc has a 100% owned subsidiary, Dry Inc., that is resident overseas. Dry Inc. sells kitchen equipment that has been manufactured by Wash plc. The results of Dry Inc. for the year ended 31 March 2005 are as follows:

		£	£
Trading profit			580,000
Corporation tax			160,000
			420,000
Dividend paid	– Net	270,000	
	– Withholding tax	30,000	
			300,000
Retained profits			120,000

Dry Inc.'s dividend was paid during the year ended 31 March 2005. The company's corporation tax liability for the year ended 31 March 2005 was £8,000 more than that provided for in the accounts.

All of the above figures are in pounds Sterling.

Required

(a) Explain the difference between withholding tax and underlying tax in respect of an overseas dividend, and state the conditions that must be met for double taxation relief to be available in each case.   (4 marks)

(b) Calculate Wash plc's corporation tax liability for the year ended 31 March 2005.
                                                                                      (7 marks)

(c) Explain the tax implications if Wash plc were to invoice Dry Inc. for the exported kitchen equipment at a price that was less than the market price.   (4 marks)

                                                                                      (15 marks)

20   PREPARATION QUESTION: GROUP RELIEF

P Ltd owns the following holdings in ordinary shares in other companies, which are all UK resident.

Q Ltd	83%
R Ltd	77%
S Ltd	67%
M Ltd	80%

The ordinary shares of P Ltd are owned to the extent of 62% by Mr C, who also owns 70% of the ordinary shares of T Ltd, another UK resident company. In each case, the other conditions for claiming group relief, where appropriate, are satisfied. No dividends were paid by the companies during the year in question.

The following are the results of the above companies for the year ended 31 March 2005.

	M Ltd	P Ltd	Q Ltd	R Ltd	S Ltd	T Ltd
	£	£	£	£	£	£
Income						
Trading profit	10,000	0	64,000	260,000	0	70,000
Trading loss	0	223,000	0	0	8,000	0
Schedule A	0	6,000	4,000	0	0	0
Charges paid						
Gift aid donation	4,000	4,500	2,000	5,000	0	0

Required

(a) Compute the MCT payable for the above accounting period by each of the above companies, assuming group relief is claimed, where appropriate, in the most efficient manner.

(b) Advise the board of P Ltd of the advantages of increasing its holding in S Ltd, a company likely to sustain trading losses for the next two years before becoming profitable.

Guidance notes

1 Group relief questions nearly always require you to show the most efficient use of relief. You must work out the profits of each company involved, and consider the marginal tax rate of each company. Any company with small companies' marginal relief will have a marginal rate (for FY 2004) of 32.75%. Any company with starting rate marginal relief will have a marginal rate of 23.75% for FY 2004.

2 Before working out the rates of tax, you must find the lower and upper limits for small companies rate, the starting rate and marginal relief. These depend on the number of companies under common control.

3 You must also remember that eligibility for group relief depends not on common control, but on a 75% effective interest.

21 PREPARATION QUESTION: CORRESPONDING ACCOUNTING PERIODS

Harry Ltd owns 80% of the ordinary share capital of Sid Ltd. Neither company has any other associated companies and both companies have been trading since 1987.

The following information relates to the two most recent accounting periods of each company.

Harry Ltd	*12 months to*	*9 months to*
	31.12.03	*30.9.04*
Income	£	£
Schedule D Case I/(loss)	25,000	(45,000)
Schedule A	3,000	4,000
Charges paid		
Gift aid donation	2,000	2,000

Sid Ltd	*12 months to*	*12 months to*
	31.3.04	*31.3.05*
Income	£	£
Schedule D Case I	52,000	250,000
Schedule D Case III	8,000	10,000
Charges paid		
Gift aid donation	5,000	5,000

No dividends were paid by either company in the periods concerned.

Required

Compute the MCT payable by each company for each of the above accounting periods and show any loss carried forward by Harry Ltd on the assumption that Harry Ltd surrenders as much of its loss to Sid Ltd as is permitted and Harry Ltd does not make any claim to set its loss against its own profits.

Guidance notes

1   The general rule for group relief is that the profits and the losses which are to be matched up must have arisen at the same time.

2   To apply this rule where companies do not have matching accounting periods, time-apportionment must be used to work out the profits and losses of each period covered by accounting periods of the two companies. Time-apportionment is not, however, used when a company joins or leaves a group if the result would be unjust or unreasonable.

3   You may find the following table helpful.

Common period	Harry Ltd	Sid Ltd
1.1.04 – 31.3.04	(1.1.04 – 30.9.04) × 3/9	(1.4.03 – 31.3.04) × 3/12
1.4.04 – 30.9.04	(1.1.04 – 30.9.04) × 6/9	(1.4.04 – 31.3.05) × 6/12

22   APPLE LTD (PILOT PAPER)   *27 mins*

Apple Ltd owns 100% of the ordinary share capital of Banana Ltd and Cherry Ltd. The results of each company for the year ended 31 March 2005 are as follows:

	Apple Ltd £	Banana Ltd £	Cherry Ltd £
Tax adjusted Schedule DI profit/(loss)	(125,000)	650,000	130,000
Capital gain/(loss)	188,000	(8,000)	–

Apple Ltd's capital gain arose from the sale of a freehold warehouse on 15 April 2004 for £418,000. Cherry Ltd purchased a freehold office building for £290,000 on 10 January 2005.

Required

(a)   Explain the group relationship that must exist in order that group relief can be claimed.   (3 marks)

(b)   Explain how group relief should be allocated between the respective claimant companies in order to maximise the potential benefit obtained from the relief.(4 marks)

(c)   Assuming that reliefs are claimed in the most favourable manner, calculate the corporation tax liabilities of Apple Ltd, Banana Ltd and Cherry Ltd for the year ended 31 March 2005.   (8 marks)

(15 marks)

23   ALPHABETIC LTD   *27 mins*

(a) Alphabetic Ltd makes up annual accounts to 30 September. It paid four quarterly instalments of corporation tax of £156,000 each in respect of the accounting period to 30 September 2004. These were paid on 14 April 2004, 14 July 2004, 14 October 2004 and 14 January 2005. It subsequently transpired that the actual liability for the period was £800,000 and the balance of £176,000 was subsequently paid on 1 July 2005.

Alphabetic Ltd has always paid corporation tax at the full rate.

Required

State the amounts on which interest will be charged in respect of the above accounting period and the dates from which it will run.   **(4 marks)**

(b) You are required to state what action a company should take if it does not receive a corporation tax return and the penalty for not taking such action.   **(2 marks)**

(c) You are required to state:

     (i)   the fixed rate penalties for failing to submit a corporation tax return on time; and   **(4 marks)**

     (ii)   the tax-geared penalties for failing to submit a corporation tax return on time.

                                                                     (3 marks)

Your answers to (c)(i) and (c)(ii) should indicate under what circumstances these penalties are triggered.

(d) Large companies must normally pay their corporation tax liability by instalments. State the circumstances in which such a company does not need to make instalment payments.   **(2 marks)**

                                                                             (15 marks)

24   PREPARATION QUESTION: COMPUTING VAT DUE

A company which is registered for VAT but does not use the cash accounting scheme has the following transactions in the quarter from July to September 2004. All amounts exclude any VAT.

	£
Bought computers for resale	130,000
Sold computers	210,000
Bought books about computers	9,300
Sold books about computers	8,400
Wrote off a bad debt in respect of a standard rated sale for which payment was due in January 2004	4,000

The sales of computers are stated at their full value before any settlement discount. However, £20,000 of the sales were subject to a 5% discount for payment within 30 days. The discount was taken up in respect of half of those sales.

Required

Calculate the VAT due on 31 October 2004.

Guidance notes

1   First identify the standard rated purchases and sales, and the zero rated purchases and sales.

2   Then consider the effect of the settlement discount. Does it matter whether it is taken up?

3   Then compute the VAT on standard rated purchases and sales.

4   Finally, VAT will have been accounted for on the sale in January. Is any relief available?

25   NEWCOMER LTD, ONGOING LTD AND AU REVOIR LTD   *27 mins*

(a) Newcomer Ltd commenced trading on 1 October 2004. Its forecast sales are as follows.

		£
2004	October	11,500
	November	14,200
	December	21,400
2005	January	12,300
	February	14,700
	March	15,200

The company's sales are all standard rated, and the above figures are exclusive of VAT.

Required

Explain when Newcomer Ltd will be required to compulsorily register for VAT.

(4 marks)

(b) Ongoing Ltd is registered for VAT, and its sales are all standard rated. The following information relates to the company's VAT return for the quarter ended 30 September 2004:

(1)   Standard rated sales amounted to £120,000. Ongoing Ltd offers its customers a 5% discount for prompt payment, and this discount is taken by half of the customers.

(2)   Standard rated purchases and expenses amounted to £35,640. This figure includes £480 for entertaining customers.

(3)   On 15 September 2004 the company wrote off bad debts of £2,000 and £840 in respect of invoices due for payment on 10 February and 5 May 2004 respectively.

(4)   On 30 September 2004 the company purchased a motor car at a cost of £16,450 for the use of a salesperson, and machinery at a cost of £21,150. Both these figures are inclusive of VAT. The motor car is used for both business and private mileage.

Unless stated otherwise, all of the above figures are exclusive of VAT. Ongoing Ltd does not operate the cash accounting scheme.

Required

Calculate the amount of VAT payable by Ongoing Ltd for the quarter ended 30 September 2004.   (8 marks)

(c) Au Revoir Ltd has been registered for VAT since 1994, and its sales are all standard rated. The company has recently seen a downturn in its business activities, and sales for the years ended 31 October 2004 and 2005 are forecast to be £55,000 and £47,500 respectively. Both of these figures are exclusive of VAT.

Required

Explain why Au Revoir Ltd will be permitted to voluntarily deregister for VAT, and from what date registration will be effective.   (3 marks)

(15 marks)

26   SELF ASSESSMENT FOR INDIVIDUALS

27 mins

(a)   You are required to state the latest date by which an individual taxpayer should submit the tax return if:

   (i)   he wishes the Revenue to calculate his income tax liability; and

   (ii)   he wishes to calculate his own liability.   (4 marks)

(b)   You are required to state:

   (i)   the normal dates of payment of Schedule DI and II income tax for a sole trader in respect of the fiscal year 2004/05; and

   (ii)   how the amounts of these payments are arrived at.   (5 marks)

(c)   You are required to state the circumstances in which a payment on account is not required to be made by a taxpayer.   (2 marks)

(d)   You are required to state:

   (i)   the fixed penalties for late submission of tax returns and when they apply;

   (ii)   the circumstances under which the penalties will be reduced; and

   (iii)   the further penalties which may be imposed where the Revenue believe that the fixed penalties will not result in the submission of the return.   (4 marks)

(15 marks)

27   ENQUIRIES AND DETERMINATIONS

27 mins

The Revenue have to give written notice before the commencement of an enquiry into the completeness and accuracy of a self-assessment tax return.

Required

(a)   State the date by which this written notice must normally be issued;   (1 mark)

(b)   State the circumstances under which the Revenue can extend the deadline in (a) within which an enquiry may be commenced together with the relevant time limits;

                                                                    (5 marks)

(c)   State the three main reasons for the commencement of an enquiry;   (3 marks)

(d)   State what choices are open to the taxpayer where he has been notified by the Revenue that there is an additional liability as a result of an enquiry; and   (2 marks)

(e)   State what is meant by a determination and the time limit for making one.   (4 marks)

(15 marks)

28   MADELAINE AND OTTO

27 mins

(a) Madelaine has for many years been in business as a furniture and carpet retailer. Her trading and profit and loss account for the year ended 31 March 2005 is as follows.

	£	£
Sales		89,323
Opening stock	26,544	
Purchases	23,338	
	49,882	
Closing stock	24,628	
		(25,254)
Gross profit		64,069
Wages and national insurance	15,197	
Repairs and renewals	491	
Rent and rates	13,984	
General expenses	719	
Bad debts	955	
Depreciation of fixtures and fittings	415	
Interest	1,780	
Motor vehicle running costs	1,404	
Lighting and heating	2,954	
Re-location expenses	741	
Professional fees	645	
Subscriptions and donations	194	
		39,479
Net profit		24,590

Required

State what additional information you would need in order to calculate Madelaine's tax adjusted Schedule D Case I profit for the year ended 31 March 2005 and explain why you need it.   (9 marks)

(b) Otto is a self-employed television engineer. He commenced in business on 1 June 2001 and initially made up accounts to 30 November but has now changed his accounting date to 28 February.

Otto's recent results have been:

	£
1.6.01 – 30.11.01	7,000
1.12.01 – 30.11.02	16,000
1.12.02 – 30.11.03	19,000
1.12.03 – 28.2.05	25,000

Required

Calculate the amounts chargeable to income tax under Schedule D, Case I for the years 2001/02, 2002/03, 2003/04 and 2004/05.   (6 marks)

(15 marks)

29 MALCOLM

27 mins

(a) Malcolm started in business as a self-employed builder on 1 August 2003. His adjusted trading results, after capital allowances, were:

	£
Period ended 30.11.03	(10,000) Loss
Year ended 30.11.04	(20,000) Loss
Year ended 30.11.05	15,000 Profit

Prior to being self-employed Malcolm was employed as a builder when his earnings were:

	£
2003/04 (to 31 July 2003)	5,650
2002/03	8,000
2001/02	NIL

He received annual building society interest income of £3,040 (net) from 2002/03 onwards. In 2003/04 he realised a capital gain on the disposal of a non business asset of £8,400 after indexation but before the annual exemption. Taper relief was not available on the disposal of this non business asset.

Required

Show how Malcolm's trading losses can be utilised most effectively, giving your reasoning.

You may assume the 2004/05 rates and allowances apply to all years relevant to this question. (12 marks)

(b) You are required to state by what date(s) the claims you are proposing in part (a) should be submitted to the Revenue. (3 marks)

(15 marks)

30 JACQUELINE

27 mins

Jacqueline retired from her 'Do-it-yourself' shop on 30 September 2004. She had commenced trading on 1 May 2000 and had prepared accounts to 31 December each year.

Her adjusted profits/loss had been agreed with the Revenue as follows.

	£
Period to 31.12.00	5,000 profit
Year ended 31.12.01	8,000 profit
Year ended 31.12.02	13,000 profit
Year ended 31.12.03	10,000 profit
Period to 30.09.04	14,500 loss

Required

(a) Show the Schedule D Case I profits for 2000/01 to 2004/05 before claiming relief for the loss. (5 marks)

(b) Show the final Schedule D Case I profits for 2000/01 to 2004/05 after claiming terminal loss relief. (10 marks)

(15 marks)

31 LOSSES AND CHANGE OF ACCOUNTING DATE

27 mins

(a) A trader (a single person) has a trading loss for the year to 31 December 2004 of £18,000. He made a trading profit of £2,500 for the year to 31 December 2003. Other income, gains and losses were as follows:

	2003/04	2004/05
	£	£
Other income	2,500	2,900
Capital gains	–	26,000
Capital losses	–	2,000

Capital losses brought forward at 6 April 2003 are £4,700.

Taper relief is not due in respect of the capital gain.

His adjusted trading profits for the year to 31 December 2005 show a breakeven position.

Required

Show how the loss for the year to 31 December 2004 should be relieved, explaining your reasons and showing any trading and/or capital loss carried forward. (9 marks)

Use the rates and allowances for 2004/05 for both years.

(b) Sue is a self-employed secretary. She commenced trading on 1 September 2001 and initially made up accounts to 31 December each year. However, in 2005 she changed her accounting date to 31 March.

Sue's results have been:

	£
1.9.01 – 31.12.01	16,000
1.1.02 – 31.12.02	48,000
1.1.03 – 31.12.03	36,000
1.1.04 – 31.12.04	42,000
1.1.05 – 31.3.05	15,000

Required

Calculate the amounts chargeable to income tax for 2001/02 to 2004/05. (6 marks)

(15 marks)

32 PREPARATION QUESTION: PARTNERSHIPS

Clare and Justin commenced trading in partnership on 1 October 2001, initially sharing profits and losses as to Clare one third and Justin two thirds. They prepared their first set of accounts to 31 January 2002. Accounts were prepared to 31 January thereafter.

Malcolm joined the partnership on 1 May 2003. From this date the profit and losses were shared equally. On 31 December 2004, Justin resigned with Clare and Malcolm continuing to share profits equally. Schedule D Case I profits were as follows:

	£
1.10.01 - 31.01.02	26,400
y/e 31.01.03	60,000
y/e 31.01.04	117,000
y/e 31.01.05	108,108

Required

Calculate the amount on which each partner will be taxed in respect of the partnership profits for 2001/02 to 2004/05 inclusive. Show any overlap profits that remain unrelieved.

Guidance notes

1   You should start by dividing the profits for each period of account between the partners in accordance with the profit sharing ratio for that period.

2   Next you can work out how much profit should be taxed in each tax year. Apply the opening and closing year rules to each partner individually according to when he or she joins or leaves the partnership.

3   Each partner has their own overlap profits. These can be relieved when the partner concerned leaves the partnership (or possibly, on an earlier change of accounting date).

33   PARTNERSHIPS

27 mins

(a)   *Required*

Briefly explain the basis by which partners are assessed in respect of their share of a partnership's Schedule DI or DII profit.   (3 marks)

(b)   Anne and Betty have been in partnership since 1 January 1999 sharing profits equally. On 30 June 2004 Betty resigned as a partner, and was replaced on 1 July 2004 by Chloe. Profit continued to be shared equally. The partnership's Schedule DI profits are as follows:

	£
Year ended 31 December 2004	60,000
Year ended 31 December 2005	72,000

As at 6 April 2004 Anne and Betty each have unrelieved overlap profits of £3,000.

Required

Calculate the Schedule DI assessments of Anne, Betty and Chloe for 2004/05.   (6 marks)

(c)   Daniel and Edward have been in partnership since 6 April 1997, making up accounts to 5 April. On 31 December 2004 Edward resigned as a partner, and was replaced on 1 January 2005 by Frank. For 2004/05 the partnership made a Schedule DII loss of £40,000, and this has been allocated between the partners as follows.

	£
Daniel	20,000
Edward	15,000
Frank	5,000

Each of the partners has investment income. None of them have any capital gains.

Required

State the possible ways in which Daniel, Edward and Frank can relieve their Schedule DII trading losses for 2004/05.   (6 marks)

(15 Marks)

34 PREPARATION QUESTION: STAKEHOLDER PENSIONS

Bill, who was born on 18 August 1961, became a self employed medical consultant on 1 June 2004. Bill forecasts that he will have the following net relevant earnings from 2004/05.

	£
2004/05	25,000
2005/06	80,000
2006/07	60,000
2007/08	70,000
2008/09	75,000
2009/10	66,000
2010/11	70,000
2011/12	60,000

Bill has decided to contribute to a stakeholder pension scheme.

Required

(a) Calculate the maximum amount of gross pension contributions for which Bill will be entitled to tax relief in 2004/05 to 2011/12.

(b) Explain how tax relief is given for personal pension payments.

Assume the relevant rules and allowances in 2004/05 remain unchanged.

Guidance notes

1   First choose a basis year for each year. The basis year can be the year concerned or any one of the five previous tax years.

2   The relevant percentage depends on the taxpayer's age at the start of the tax year concerned.

35 PREPARATION QUESTION: PERSONAL COMPUTATION

Roger Thesaurus, a widower aged 46 on 1 June 2004, has the following income and outgoings for the tax year 2004/05.

		£	
(a)	Share of partnership profits	56,000	
(b)	Interest on a deposit account with the Scotia Bank	1,197	(net)
(c)	Interest paid on a loan taken out to purchase an interest in the partnership of which Mr Thesaurus is a partner.	6,000	(amount paid)
(d)	Personal pension contributions. Roger joined a stakeholder pension scheme on 6.4.04. Roger chose 1999/00 as his basis year in 2004/05. In 1999/00 partnership profits were £80,000	11,700	(amount paid)
(e)	Dividends received on UK shares	900	(amount received)

Required

(a) Calculate the income tax payable by Mr Thesaurus for 2004/05.

(b) Explain how you have dealt with the personal pension contribution and the interest paid on the loan to purchase a share in the partnership.

Guidance notes

1   The major part of this question requires you to calculate an individual's overall tax position. You should start by heading your answer and laying it out: non-savings, savings (excl dividend) and dividend income. Next show charges, total income and the personal allowance. It will then be more difficult to overlook anything.

2   Start with non-savings income and any deductions made specifically from it.

3   Insert the types of savings (excl dividend) and dividend income, remembering that amounts are always included gross in the tax computation even if the amounts are actually received net.

4   Deduct any charges on income. Firstly from non-savings income, then from savings (excl dividend) income and lastly from dividend income.

5   Total income less charges is statutory total income or STI. This is an important figure in some computations, particularly those involving losses.

6   After deducting the personal allowance to find the taxable income, you need to calculate tax payable. Don't forget to extend the basic rate band by the gross amount of the pension contributions paid.

36   LAI CHAN

45 mins

Until 31 December 2004 Lai Chan was employed by Put-it-Right plc as a management consultant. The following information relates to the period of employment from 6 April to 31 December 2004.

(1)   Lai was paid a gross salary of £3,250 per month.

(2)   She contributed 6% of her gross salary into Put-it-right plc's Revenue approved occupational pension scheme. The company contributed a further 6%.

(3)   Put-it-Right plc provided Lai with a 2600 cc motor car with a list price of £26,400. The motor car's CO_2 emissions were 195g/km. Lai paid Put-it-Right plc £130 per month for the use of the motor car.

Put-it-Right plc paid for the petrol in respect of all the mileage done by Lai during 2004/05. She paid the company £30 per month towards the cost of her private petrol.

The motor car was returned to Put-it-Right plc on 31 December 2004.

(4)   Put-it-Right plc provided Lai with an interest free loan of £30,000 on 1 January 2000. She repaid £20,000 of the loan on 30 June 2004 with the balance of £10,000 being repaid on 31 December 2004. The loan was not used for a qualifying purposes.

On 1 January 2005 Lai commenced in self-employment running a music recording studio. The following information relates to the period of self-employment from 1 January to 5 April 2005.

(1)   The Schedule DII profit for the period 1 January to 5 April 2005 is £19,900. This figure is *before* taking account of capital allowances.

(2)   Lai purchased the following assets:

1 January 2005	Recording equipment	£9,300
15 January 2005	Motor car	£14,800
20 February 2005	Motor car	£10,400
4 March 2005	Recording equipment	£2,600

The motor car purchased on 15 January 2005 for £14,800 is used by Lai, and 40% of the mileage is for private purposes. The motor car purchased on 20 February 2005 for £10,400 is used by an employee, and 10% of the mileage is for private purposes.

The recording equipment purchased on 4 March 2005 for £2,600 is to be treated as a short-life asset.

(3) Since becoming self-employed Lai has paid £390 (net) per month into a stakeholder pension scheme. Payments are made on the 20th of each month.

(4) Lai Chan is single and does not have any children.

Required

(a) Calculate Lai's income tax liability for 2004/05.   (20 marks)

(b) Briefly explain how Lai's income tax liability for 2004/05 will be paid to the Revenue.
(5 marks)

(25 marks)

37   CLAYTON DELANEY   *47 mins*

Clayton Delaney, who is now aged 59, had been a self-employed electrician for many years. His business was centred on a shop from which he sold electrical goods to the public and to the electrical trade. He also carried out electrical work himself for his customers.

Because of deteriorating health his wife could no longer look after the shop in Clayton's absence and she retired aged 60 on 31 March 2004. She had no source of income thereafter. Clayton decided to permanently cease trading on 30 June 2004 and on 1 July 2004 commenced working for a firm of electrical contractors.

His summarised accounts for the year ended 30 June 2004 are as follows.

Profit and loss account

		£		£
Telephone	(1)	240	Gross profits on sales	19,645
Repairs	(2)	1,180	Bank interest received December 2003	
Depreciation		1,350	(Note (3) of other relevant	
Buildings insurance	(3)	600	information)	300
Lighting and heating	(3)	420	Profit on sale of shop fittings	20
Car expenses	(4)	1,750	Work done for customers	16,000
Bad debts	(5)	950		
Rates	(6)	1,850		
Wages and national insurance contributions:				
Mrs Delaney	(7)	5,000		
Wages and national insurance contributions:				
Mr Delaney		11,850		
Bank interest paid	(8)	630		
General expenses	(9)	1,995		
Net profit		8,150		
		35,965		35,965

Figures in brackets refers to notes to the accounts.

Notes to the accounts

(1) Telephone: one-fifth of the charge is for private calls.

(2) Repairs were as follows (see also note (3)).

	£
Roof repairs	650
Redecorating bedroom	230
Replacing floor tiles in shop	300
	1,180

(3) Clayton and his wife live on the shop premises. The Revenue have agreed that two-thirds of the household expenditure is in respect of the living accommodation.

(4) Car expenses: the total mileage in the year was 16,000 of which half was private. This was the same fraction as in earlier years.

(5) **Bad debts**

	£		£
Trade debts written off	300	Specific debt provision b/f	300
Loan to neighbour written off	500	Recovery of trade debt	
Specific debt provision c/f	800	previously written off	350
		Profit and loss account	950
	1,600		1,600

(6) **Rates**

	£
Business rates	1,200
Council tax	650
	1,850

(7) Mrs Delaney's wages: Mrs Delaney looked after the shop in Mr Delaney's absence and ran the clerical side of the business.

(8) Bank interest paid: the interest was paid on the business account overdraft.

(9) **General expenses**

	£
Accountancy	600
Legal costs in defending claim for allegedly faulty work	200
Printing, stationery and postage	220
Gifts to trade customers: one Christmas hamper each, costing £30	900
Donation of prize in local carnival (a free advertisement was provided in the programme)	50
Donation to a national charity (not paid under the gift aid scheme)	25
	1,995

(10) Overlap profits on commencement of trade were £1,200.

In addition Clayton had taken stock from the shop for personal use. The cost price of these items was £600 and the average gross profit margin was 20%. No payment had been made for the goods by Clayton.

The tax written-down values at 1 July 2003 of business assets were as follows.

Car	£5,700
Pool	£490

On 31 December 2003 Clayton traded in his car for £4,500 and purchased a new one costing £9,000.

On 30 June 2004 the items in the pool were sold for £400 (all less than original cost) and the car had a market value of £3,500.

Other relevant information is as follows.

(1) Clayton earned £1,433.33 gross per month, payable on the last day of the month in arrears. Because he was expected to travel around in his employment he was provided with a company car by his employer.

(2) The car had a diesel engine and had a list price of £10,000 when new. Its CO_2 emissions were 152g/km. Clayton's employer agreed to provide fuel for the first 5,000 miles of his private motoring during 2004/05.

(3) Clayton has an investment account with the Halifax Bank. Interest of £395 was credited on 31 December 2004.

(4) Clayton had purchased a life annuity and received a monthly gross amount of £100 on the first of each month commencing 1 September 2004. The capital element of the payment was agreed by the Revenue to be £50 per month. The income element of the annuity was received net of 20% tax.

Required

(a) Calculate the amount of the taxable profits for 2004/05.   (19 marks)

(b) Calculate the amount of Clayton's income tax payable for 2004/05.   (7 marks)

(26 marks)

38   MARK KETT   *45 mins*

On 30 September 2004 Mark Kett ceased trading as a marketing consultant. He had been self-employed since 1 July 1999. On 1 October 2004 Mark commenced employment as the marketing manager of Sleep-Easy plc. The company runs a hotel. The following information is available for 2004/05:

Self-employment

(1) Mark has tax adjusted Schedule DII profits of £57,600 for the year ended 30 June 2004, and profits of £17,400 for the three month period to 30 September 2004. These figures are before taking account of capital allowances.

(2) The tax written down values for capital allowances purposes at 1 July 2003 are as follows:

	£
General pool	43,800
Expensive motor car	24,900

The expensive motor car is used by Mark, and 40% of the mileage is for private purposes.

(3) On 15 August 2003 Mark purchased office furniture for £8,900. All of the items included in the general pool were sold for £43,200 on 30 September 2004. On the cessation of trading Mark personally retained the expensive motor car. Its value on 30 September 2004 was £15,400.

(4) Mark has unused overlap profits brought forward of £9,800.

(5) Mark's business is a small enterprise for capital allowance purposes.

Employment

(1) Mark is paid a salary of £6,250 per month by Sleep-Easy plc, from which income tax of £1,890 per month has been deducted under PAYE.

(2) During the period from 1 October 2004 to 5 April 2005 Mark used his private motor car for business purposes. He drove 10,000 miles in the performance of his duties for Sleep-Easy plc, for which the company paid an allowance of 20 pence per mile. The relevant Revenue statutory mileage rates to be used as the basis of an expense claim are 40 pence per mile for the first 10,000 miles, and 25 pence per mile thereafter.

(3) On 1 October 2004 Sleep-Easy plc provided Mark with an interest free loan of £60,000 so that he could purchase a new main residence. The official Revenue rate of interest was 5%.

(4) During the period from 1 October 2004 to 5 April 2005 Mark was provided with free meals in Sleep-Easy plc's staff canteen. The total cost of these meals to the company was £1,200.

Other information

(1) During 2004/05 Mark received dividends of £2,880 (net).

(2) Mark's payments on account of income tax in respect of 2004/05 totalled £24,400.

Required

(a) Calculate Mark's assessment under Schedule DII for 2004/05. You should prepare separate capital allowance computations for each period of account. (10 marks)

(b) Calculate the income tax payable by Mark for 2004/05, and the balancing payment or repayment that will be due for that tax year. (12 marks)

(c) Advise Mark as to how long he must retain the records used in preparing his tax return for 2004/05, and the potential consequences of not retaining the records for the required period. (3 marks)

(25 marks)

39 **PREPARATION QUESTION: A COTTAGE AND SHARES**

John Hammond, a single man aged 60, had employment income of £8,000, dividend income of £16,200 net and had the following transactions in the year ended 5 April 2005.

(a) On 5 May 2004 he sold his holiday cottage in Scotland for £100,000. The legal and advertising expenses of the sale were £800.

John had purchased the property on 5 September 1982 for £25,000 and had incurred costs of £8,000 on 1 December 1983 for the building of an extension.

The indexed cost of the original property at April 1998 was £49,625, and the indexed cost of the extension at the same date was £14,968.

(b) On 14 September 2004 he sold 4,000 shares in JVD Products plc for £40,000, his previous transactions being as follows.

12 June 1986 purchased 700 shares cost £3,000 (indexed cost at April 98 = £4,988)
12 May 2001 purchased 2,800 shares cost £12,000
12 August 2003 purchased 500 shares cost £2,000

The shares are a non-business asset for taper relief purposes.

Required

Compute the income tax and capital gains tax liabilities of John Hammond for the year 2004/05.

Guidance notes

1   Individuals do not get an indexation allowance after 6 April 1998. Instead they may be eligible for taper relief.

2   Shares acquired after 6.4.98 are not pooled. They are matched with disposals on a LIFO basis. In the exam you will not be expected to calculate the indexation allowance for an individual.

3   When you come to work out the tax liabilities, remember that income and gains share the starting and basic rate bands. Income is dealt with first then any gains in the starting rate band are taxed at 10%. Any gains in the basic rate band are taxed at 20%. Gains that fall into the higher rate band are taxed at 40%.

40   YVONNE, SALLY AND JOANNE   *27 mins*

(a)   Yvonne had the following transactions in the shares of Scotia plc. The shares are a non business asset for taper relief purposes.

		Shares	£
18 August 1995	bought	3,000	6,000
19 September 2002	bought	2,000	5,000
13 March 2005	sold	5,000	23,000
28 March 2005	bought	1,000	4,400

The indexed value of shares in the 1985 Pool at 5 April 1998 is £6,510.

You are required to calculate Yvonne's capital gain for 2004/05.   (8 marks)

(b)   In 2004/05 Sally's capital gains tax position was as follows.

	£
Capital gain on a business asset (acquired October 2001)	40,000
Capital gain on non-business asset (acquired May 2003)	10,000
Capital loss arising in year	6,000
Capital loss brought forward	12,000

Required

Show how the losses should be allocated to obtain the maximum tax advantage and calculate any gain chargeable.   (4 marks)

(c)   Joanne bought a warehouse for use in her business on 1 August 2002. She used it until 1 August 2003 and then let it out until she sold it on 1 February 2005. Her gain on sale was £50,000.

Required

Show Joanne's gain after taper relief.   (3 marks)

41 JACK CHAN

27 mins

Jack Chan, aged 45, has been in business as a sole trader since 1 May 1999. On 28 February 2005 he transferred the business to his daughter Jill, at which time the following assets were sold to her:

(1) Goodwill with a market value of £60,000. The goodwill has been built up since 1 May 1999, and has a nil cost. Jill paid Jack £50,000 for the goodwill.

(2) A freehold office building with a market value of £130,000. The office building was purchased on 1 July 2004 for £110,000, and has always been used by Jack for business purposes. Jill paid Jack £105,000 for the office building.

(3) A freehold warehouse with a market value of £140,000. The warehouse was purchased on 1 September 2002 for £95,000, and has never been used by Jack for business purposes. Jill paid Jack £135,000 for the warehouse.

(4) A motor car with a market value of £25,000. The motor car was purchased on 1 November 2003 for £23,500, and has always been used by Jack for business purposes. Jill paid Jack £20,000 for the motor car.

Where possible, Jack and Jill have elected to hold over any gains arising. Jack's taxable income for 2004/05 is £23,600. He has unused capital losses of £6,400 brought forward from 2003/04.

Required

Calculate Jack's Capital gains tax liability for 2004/05, and advise him by when this should be paid. **(15 marks)**

42 MR EDWARDS

27 mins

A client, Mr Edwards, has made an appointment to discuss his VAT position with you on 10 December 2004. He started in business making hand-made ladies' shoes on 1 April 2004. His monthly turnover figures to date are:

	£
April	7,694
May	5,326
June	7,295
July	7,314
August	9,405
September	10,792
October	10,977
November	11,291

Turnover is expected to continue to increase. Mr Edwards is concerned that he should now be charging customers VAT and is seeking your advice about registration.

He has heard that if he has to register for VAT he can submit an annual return to cut down on administration.

He would welcome your advice on both these matters.

Required

Prepare notes for your meeting with Mr Edwards. **(15 marks)**

43   PREPARATION QUESTION: BENEFITS

You have been asked to assist in the completion of forms P11D in respect of the directors of your company for the year 2004/05.

The following benefits are enjoyed by various directors.

(a)   A director has had the use of a private house bought by the company for £120,000 in 2000. The director paid all of the house expenses plus the agreed open market annual rental of £2,000. The annual value of the house is £2,000.

(b)   A television video system, which had been provided at the start of 2000/01 for the use of a director and which had cost the company £3,500, was taken over by the director on 6 April 2004 for a payment of £600 (its market value at that date).

(c)   A director has a loan of £4,000 at 4% interest to enable him to purchase his annual season ticket. This is the only loan he had taken out.

(d)   Medical insurance premiums were paid for a director and his family, under a group scheme, at a cost to the company of £800. Had the director paid for this as an individual the cost would have been £1,400.

(e)   On 6 September 2004 a director was given the use of a Mercedes car which had cost £24,000. The CO_2 emissions of the car were 245g/km. The director used the Mercedes for both business and private purposes. The company paid for all fuel while the car was provided.

(f)   On 6 April 2004 the company lent a director a computer costing £3,900 for use at home. The director used the computer for both business and private purposes.

Required

Show how each of the above benefits would be quantified for inclusion in the forms P11D. Assume that the official rate of interest is 5%.

Guidance notes

1   Work through each benefit separately. Calculate its value before you move on to the next benefit. Watch out for exempt benefits.

2   Remember that any benefit that is only available for part of a year must be time apportioned. This is often the case in exam questions with car and fuel benefits. Is it relevant here?

3   The rules for the calculation of car and fuel benefits are extremely topical.

44 RITA

27 mins

Rita, who is a fashion designer for Daring Designs Limited, was re-located from London to Manchester on 6 April 2004. Her annual salary is £48,000. She was immediately provided with a house with an annual value of £4,000 for which her employer paid an annual rent of £3,500. Rita was re-imbursed relevant re-location expenditure of £12,000. Daring Designs Limited provided ancillary services for the house in 2004/05 as follows.

	£
Electricity	700
Gas	1,200
Water	500
Council tax	1,300
Property repairs	3,500

The house has been furnished by Daring Designs Limited prior to Rita's occupation at a cost of £30,000. On 6 October 2004 Rita bought all of the furniture from Daring Designs Ltd for £20,000 when its market value was £25,000.

Daring Designs Limited had made an interest free loan to Rita in 2003 of £10,000. The loan is not being used for a 'qualifying purpose'. No part of the loan has been repaid.

Rita was provided with a company car. It had a list price of £18,500 and a CO_2 emissions figure of 149g/km. Daring Designs Limited paid for the petrol for all the mileage done by Rita until 5 December 2004. On 5 December 2004 the company discontinued the company car scheme and sold the car to Rita for £5,000, its market value on that date.

Required

Calculate the total amount chargeable to income tax as employment income on Rita for the year 2004/05.

(15 marks)

45 JOSEPHINE

27 mins

Josephine, who is not contracted out of the state pension scheme, receives a weekly salary of £402. Josephine is provided with a company car by her employer. Until 5 December 2004 the car was a diesel car with CO_2 emissions of 181g/km. The original list price of this car was £12,000. On 6 December 2004 the car was exchanged for a new petrol car with a list price of £21,000 and a CO_2 emissions figure of 148g/km. Josephine's employer provided fuel for both cars for both business and private motoring.

Josephine also received the benefit of medical insurance at the cost of £500 to her employer. Her employer also paid £10,000 to a private nursery for places for Josephine's two small children under a contract between the employer and the nursery.

Required

Calculate the national insurance contributions payable by Josephine and her employer for the year 2004/05. Weekly NIC limits – earnings threshold £91; upper earnings limit £610.

(15 marks)

46   APPLEBY PIES   *27 mins*

Juliet Appleby runs a business making fancy cakes for birthdays and celebrations. The business employs two part time bakers and is run out of a converted garage in the garden of Juliet's home in Anglesea.

Since setting up a website two years ago Juliet has found her turnover has doubled due to a vast increase in mail order sales. This has also resulted in Juliet registering for VAT.

Juliet has arranged a meeting with you to discuss the impact on her sole trader business of converting to limited company status.

Required

Prepare brief notes for your meeting with Juliet under the following headings;

(i)   Income tax   (3 marks)
(ii) Capital allowances   (3 marks)
(iii) Trading losses   (3 marks)
(iv) Capital gains tax   (3 marks)
(v)   VAT   (3 marks)

                                                    (15 marks)

47   JANE JONES   *27 mins*

Jane Jones has the choice of two alternative offers of employment. Regardless of which alternative is chosen, she will commence employment on 6 April 2004 (you should assume that today's date is 15 March 2004) and will drive 10,000 miles during 2004/05 in the performance of her duties.

Aurora plc

Under the offer of employment from Aurora plc, Jane will receive a salary of £30,000. On 6 April 2004 Aurora plc will provide Jane with a new 1300 cc motor car with a list price of £18,400. The CO_2 emissions of the car are 182g/km. The company will pay for all running costs, including private petrol. Jane will pay Aurora plc £50 per month for the use of the motor car. Under this alternative Jane will not run a private motor car.

Zodiac plc

Under the offer of employment from Zodiac plc, Jane will receive a salary of £32,000. From 6 April 2004 she will use her private motor car for business mileage, for which Zodiac plc will pay an allowance of 20 pence per mile. The Revenue authorised mileage rates to be used as a basis of an expense claim are 40 pence per mile for the first 10,000 miles, and 25 pence per mile thereafter. Jane's total annual cost of running her private motor car, including leasing costs and fuel, will be £7,100.

Required

(a) Calculate Jane's income tax liability for 2004/05 if she:

    (i)   Accepts the offer of employment from Aurora plc.   (5 marks)

    (ii)   Accepts the offer of employment from Zodiac plc.   (5 marks)

(b) Advise Jane as to which offer of employment is the more beneficial. Your answer should be supported by a calculation of the amount of income, net of income tax, that she will receive for 2004/05 under each alternative offer of employment. NIC should be ignored.   (5 marks)

(15 marks)

48   CAROL COURIER

27 mins

For the purposes of this question you should assume that today's date is 15 March 2004.

Carol Courier is employed by Quick-Speed plc as a delivery driver, and is paid a salary of £26,000 p.a. She contributes 5% of her gross salary into Quick-Speed plc's Revenue approved occupational pension scheme.

As an alternative to being employed, Quick-Speed plc have offered Carol the opportunity to work for the company on a self-employed basis. The details of the proposed arrangement for the year ended 5 April 2005 are as follows:

(1) Carol will commence being self-employed on 6 April 2004.

(2) Her income from Quick-Speed plc is expected to be £38,000.

(3) When not working for Quick-Speed plc, Carol will be allowed to work for other clients. Her income from this work is expected to be £8,500.

(4) Carol will lease a delivery van from Quick-Speed plc, and 100% of the mileage will be for business purposes. The cost of leasing and running the delivery van will be £4,400.

(5) When she is unavailable Carol will have to provide a replacement driver to deliver for Quick-Speed plc. This will cost her £2,800.

(6) Carol will contribute £2,000 (gross) into a personal pension scheme during 2004/05. This will provide her with the same benefits as the occupational pension scheme provided by Quick-Speed plc.

Required

(a) Assuming that Carol does not accept the offer from Quick-Speed plc and continues to be employed by the company, calculate her income tax and Class 1 NIC liability for 2004/05.   (5 marks)

(b) Assuming that Carol accepts the offer to work for Quick-Speed plc on a self-employed basis from 6 April 2004 onwards, calculate her income tax, Class 2 NIC and Class 4 NIC liability for 2004/05.   (6 marks)

(c) Advise Carol as to whether it will be beneficial to accept the offer to work for Quick-Speed plc on a self-employed basis. Your answer should be supported by a calculation of the amount by which Carol's income for 2004/05 (net of outgoings, income tax and NIC) will increase or decrease if she accepts the offer.   (4 marks)

(15 marks)

49   MR ROYLE   *27 mins*

Your client, Mr Royle, is considering acquiring the business of a local company. The company has previously been profitable but has made losses in the last two years due to the ill-health of the managing director, who is also the main shareholder. Mr Royle is sure that he can turn the business around and make it profitable again. The company owns various items of machinery and a factory.

Mr Royle is considering either buying the assets of the company or buying the whole of the shares in the company. He was made redundant by his employer last year and received a large cash payment which he will be using to buy the business.

Required

Write a letter to Mr Royle outlining the advantages and disadvantages of buying:

(a)   the assets of the business; or   (8 marks)
(b)   the shares in the company.   (7 marks)

(15 marks)

50   ABDUL PATEL   *27 mins*

Abdul Patel is to commence in business on 1 April 2004 running a retail shop (you should assume that today's date is 15 March 2004).

His tax adjusted Schedule DI profit for the year ended 31 March 2005 is expected to be £80,000.

Abdul is unsure whether he should run his business as a sole trader or via a limited company. If the business is run as a limited company it will be called AP Ltd, and Abdul will personally withdraw £45,000 of the company's profits. This will be either as:

1   Director's remuneration (the gross remuneration will be £45,000), or

2   Dividends (the figure actually withdrawn will be £45,000).

The following information is also available:

1   For 2004/05 Abdul's investment income will fully utilise his personal allowance and 10% tax band, and partly utilise the basic rate tax band.

2   Abdul will have £25,000 of the basic rate tax band unused for 2004/05.

Required

(a)   Calculate Abdul's liability to income tax, Class 2 NIC and Class 4 NIC for 2004/05 if he runs his business as a sole trader. You are not expected to calculate the tax liability on Abdul's investment income.   (4 marks)

(b)   Assuming that Abdul incorporates his business on 1 April 2004, calculate the corporation tax liability of AP Ltd for the year ended 31 March 2005 and the income tax and Class 1 NIC liability of Abdul for 2004/05 if he withdraws:

   (i)   Gross director's remuneration of £45,000, or   (7 marks)

   (ii)   Net dividends of £45,000.   (4 marks)

You are not expected to calculate the tax liability on Abdul's investment income.

(15 marks)

51   INCORPORATION

27 mins

You have been asked to make a technical presentation to members of your firm on the subject of incorporation of a business.

Required

Make brief notes to be handed out at the presentation. Your notes should cover the following:

(a) income tax treatment on incorporation of business   (4 marks)
(b) capital allowances   (2 marks)
(c) trading losses   (2 marks)
(d) capital gains   (4 marks)
(e) value added tax   (3 marks)
                                                                                                                     (15 marks)

Answers

1 PREPARATION QUESTION: SUNDRY ADJUSTMENTS

> **Tutor's hint.** The factory had always been used as a factory, so you should not have discussed the effect of non-qualifying use.

(a) The gross amount of loan interest accruing during the year will be included in the company's profits chargeable to corporation tax and charged to tax at the appropriate rate. **The gross interest is taxed under Schedule D Case III on an accruals basis.**

(b) **There will be a charge to corporation tax on any capital gain.** In addition, the residue before sale must be calculated, being the cost less any industrial buildings allowances to date. **If the proceeds exceed the residue before sale a balancing charge will arise** (restricted to the amount of the allowances claimed) and will be chargeable to corporation tax. **If the proceeds are less than the residue before sale, the difference will give rise to a balancing allowance which will be added to the company's other capital allowances.**

(c) The **defalcations by the junior members of staff will be deductible** in arriving at the company's Schedule D Case I profits, provided that they are not covered by insurance. **Sums stolen by a director are not deductible** as a trading expense *(Bamford v ATA Advertising 1972)*.

(d) **Expenditure on repairs to a newly-acquired asset which cannot be used by the purchaser in its unaltered state is regarded as capital expenditure and is therefore not deductible in arriving at the company's Schedule D Case I profit** *(Law Shipping Co Ltd v CIR 1923)*. Furthermore, as the expenditure was on retail premises it will not qualify for industrial buildings allowances either.

(e) **The cost of business entertainment is not deductible** for tax purposes. **The cost of staff entertainment, on the other hand, is deductible.**

2 PREPARATION QUESTION: CAPITAL AND REVENUE

> **Tutor's hint.** The topic of this question is a basic principle of UK taxation. It would be very easy simply to write everything you know about the distinction between capital and revenue items. This would, however, be a mistake. It is important to read this sort of question carefully. You are asked how the distinction is applied to items in a company's profit and loss account, so you should consider profits as well as deductions from them, and you are specifically required to refer to relevant case law.

The distinction between capital and revenue is an essential one in the application of UK corporation tax. **Capital expenditure is not deductible in the computation of trading profits, except to the extent that it gives rise to capital allowances. Capital profits are taxed as capital gains:** although the rate of corporation tax is the same as for income, an indexation allowance is available in the computation of capital gains, and **capital losses may only be relieved against capital gains.**

Capital expenditure

Expenditure on an asset which is for the enduring benefit of the trade is capital. Thus the cost of a machine which will be used to generate profits is capital, but the cost of stock bought for resale is a revenue expense.

Legal and professional expenses associated with capital expenditure are themselves treated as capital. However, **the cost of legal advice on employment contracts and the cost of legal work on the renewal of a lease for less than 50 years are deductible** in

47

computing trading profits. The incidental costs of loan finance are deductible in that they are taken into account in computing profits and losses on loan relationships.

The most contentious items of expenditure will often be repairs (revenue expenditure) and improvements (capital expenditure). The distinction between the two is based on a number of important legal cases.

(a) **Restoration of an asset by, for instance, replacing a subsidiary part of the asset will be deductible expenditure**. It was held that expenditure on a replacement factory chimney was deductible since the chimney was a subsidiary part of the factory (*Samuel Jones & Co (Devondale) Ltd v CIR 1951*). However, in another case a football club demolished a spectators' stand and replaced it with a modern equivalent. This was held not to be repair, since repair is the restoration by renewal or replacement of subsidiary parts of a larger entity, and the stand formed a distinct and *separate* part of the club (and was thus not a *subsidiary* part of the club) (*Brown v Burnley Football and Athletic Co Ltd 1980*).

(b) **Initial repairs to improve a recently acquired asset to make it fit to earn profits will be treated as capital expenditure**. In *Law Shipping Co Ltd v CIR 1923* the taxpayer failed to obtain relief for expenditure on making a newly bought ship seaworthy prior to using it.

(c) **Initial repairs to remedy normal wear and tear of recently acquired assets will be deductible**. *Odeon Associated Theatres Ltd v Jones 1971* can be contrasted with the *Law Shipping* judgement. Odeon were allowed to deduct expenditure incurred on improving the state of recently acquired cinemas.

Where an asset is bought on hire purchase the cash cost is treated as capital, and the finance charges are treated as revenue expenditure, normally spread over the period of the hire purchase agreement. Where assets are leased, the lease payments are treated as revenue expenditure.

Capital profits

Where an asset is held to be used in the business (for example machinery) and is then sold, any profit is a capital gain. The same would apply to investments. Sales of stock in the course of trade, on the other hand, give rise to revenue profits.

3   TRUNK LTD

> **Tutor's hint.** In a question such as this, it is a good idea to tick each item on the question paper as you deal with it, so that you do not miss anything. You must also read the question carefully: you were asked to explain your treatment of items, including those not included in your computation. Did you do this?

TRUNK LIMITED
COMPUTATION OF ADJUSTED PROFIT OR LOSS

	£	£	*Note*
Loss per accounts		(42,000)	
Additions to profit			
Lease premium deduction amortisation	2,000		(a)
Depreciation	9,500		(a)
Loss on sale of lorry	6,000		(a)
Entertaining	1,800		(b)
Legal fees	4,400		(c)
General expenses	2,500		(d)
Repairs and renewals	5,000		(e)
		31,200	
		(10,800)	
Deductions from profit			
Reduction in general provision	1,000		(f)
Deemed extra rent on lease premium	1,640		(g)
Rents received	10,000		(h)
Gain on sale of plant	7,400		(a)
Capital allowances	7,160		(i)
		(27,200)	
Adjusted loss		(38,000)	

Notes

(a) **Depreciation and amortisation not deductible, being capital. Losses and gains on the sale of fixed assets** are essentially catching-up for inadequate or excessive depreciation, and **are similarly not deductible (losses) or taxable (gains).**

(b) **The cost of entertaining customers, and the cost of gifts of food to customers, are by statute not deductible.** Entertaining staff is not caught by this rule.

(c) The **legal fees in relation to the new lease are not deductible** because they are capital in nature. The **legal fees in relation to the recovery of the employee loan are not deductible** because they are not for trade purposes: the trade is manufacturing, not moneylending. **Legal fees in relation to service contracts, are, however, deductible.**

(d) **Penalties and fines are not deductible.** Course fees for trade-related training of employees, on the other hand, are deductible.

(e) **The cost of the new windows is not deductible because it is of a capital nature,** being needed to put the recently-acquired warehouse in a usable condition. Routine repairs, on the other hand, are deductible.

(f) **General provisions are not deductible, so reductions in them are not taxable.** Specific provisions, on the other hand, and actual bad debts, are deductible.

(g) **When a trader pays a lease premium, the part treated as income for the landlord is treated as extra rent payable by the trader, spread over the term of the lease.** The extra rent per year is:

£20,000 × [50 − (10 − 1)] × 2% × 1/10 = £1,640

(h) **Rents are taxed under Schedule A, not Schedule D Case I.**

(i) **Capital allowances are the statutory substitute for depreciation.**

(j) The following items require no adjustment.

(i) **Patent fees.**

(ii) **Debenture interest on a trading loan relationship**, which is **deductible** by statute.

(iii) **Discounts received, which simply affect the cost of purchases.**

(iv) **The insurance recovery for damage to stock, which simply replaces some or all of the revenue which would have been earned had the stock not been damaged.**

Marking guide

	Marks
Additions	
Lease amortisation	½
Depreciation	½
Loss on sale of lorry	½
Entertaining/food gifts	2
Legal fees	1
General expenses	1
Repairs and renewals	2
Deductions	
Bad debts	2
Lease premium	2
Rents	½
Gain on sale of plant	½
CAs	½
Patent fees	½
Debenture interest	½
Discounts	½
Insurance recovery	½
	15

---

4 SCHEDULE D ADJUSTMENTS

Tutor's hint. It was important to answer this question by giving reasons for the adjustments you made and quoting case law where appropriate.

(a)

	£	Notes	£
Profits per accounts			290,000
Add:			
Director's salary	24,000	(ii)	
Damages	12,000	(iii)	
Repairs	12,000	(iv)	
Employee loans w/o	2,000	(v)	
Goods sold abroad	40,000	(viii)	
			90,000
Deduct:			
Decrease in general bad debt provision	3,000	(vi)	
Insurance recoveries	14,000	(ix)	
			(17,000)
			363,000

Notes

(i) **The costs of seconding employees to charities are deductible,** so no adjustment needs to be made in respect of the £22,000 paid to the director seconded to Oxfam.

(ii)   **The salary paid to a director seconded to a group company** was not paid wholly and exclusively for the purpose of the company's trade so it is **not deductible** and an adjustment is needed.

(iii)   **In *Strong and Co v Woodifield 1906* damages paid were held to be non-deductible because they were too remote from the trade.** In this case disallow the net costs after insurance recoveries.

(iv)   **The cost of getting the office ready for use is non-deductible capital expenditure** (*Law Shipping Co Ltd v CIR 1923*).

(v)   **Employee loans are not made for the purposes of the company's trade so these are non-deductible.**

(vi)   **A decrease in the general bad debt provision is not taxable** so an adjustment must be made to the accounts figure. No adjustments are required in respect of specific provisions for bad debts, or in respect of bad debts written off.

(vii)   **Redundancy payments in a continuing trade are deductible provided they are paid wholly and exclusively for trade purposes.**

(viii) **The company must make a transfer pricing adjustment to adjust the price of goods sold abroad to their market value.**

(ix)   **Insurance recoveries in respect of the let properties are taxable under Schedule A.** This means that you need to make an adjustment to ensure the recoveries are not also included in the Schedule D profits.

(x)   **Insurance recoveries in respect of repairs to the general office are taxable under Schedule D so no adjustment is needed.**

Marking guide	Marks
Calculation	2
Notes:	
Secondment to charity	1
Secondment to subsidiary	1
Damages paid to customer	1
Repairs to make offices usable	1
Bad debts	3
Redundancy payments	1
Transfer pricing	2
Insurance recovery: Schedule A income	2
Insurance recovery: Schedule DI income	1
	15

5   **PREPARATION QUESTION: CORPORATION TAX COMPUTATION**

> **Tutor's hint.** This was a straightforward corporation tax computation, but you had to think carefully about the point of part (b). This tests the new rules for small companies which were introduced in Finance Act 2004 and are therefore, very topical.

(a) **Corporation tax computation for the accounting period**

	£	£
Schedule D Case I	45,000	
Trading losses brought forward	(20,000)	
		25,000
Schedule A		15,000
Schedule D Case III		4,000
Capital gains (£35,000 + £7,000)	42,000	
Less capital losses brought forward	(40,000)	
		2,000
		46,000
Less: gift aid donation		(7,000)
Profit for small companies' rate purposes		39,000
Corporation tax £39,000 × 19%	7,410	
Less small companies marginal relief £(50,000 – 39,000) × $^{19}/_{400}$	(523)	
Mainstream corporation tax		6,887

(b) If a dividend is paid to a non-corporate shareholder PCTCT equal to the amount of the dividend will be assessed to corporation tax at 19%. The company's tax liability will be increased by £268 (see working).

Working

Average tax liability prior to adjustment $\dfrac{6,887}{39,000} \times 100 = 17.66\%$

	£
Revised tax liability £(39,000 – 20,000) × 17.66%	3,355
£20,000 × 19%	3,800
	7,155

Increase in tax payable as a result of the dividend £(7,155 – 6,887) = £268

6   PREPARATION QUESTION: SMALL COMPANIES TAXATION

CAPITAL ALLOWANCES
FOR PERIOD ENDING 31 MARCH 2005

	FYA	Pool	Allowances
	£	£	£
Car for salesman (N)		7,000	
Less: WDA @ 25% x 9/12		(1,313)	1,313
		5,687	
Van	10,000		
Computer	2,000		
	12,000		
FYA @ 50%	(6,000)	6,000	6,000
Energy efficient car (N)	15,000		
FYA @ 100%	(15,000)	nil	15,000
TWDB c/f		11,687	
Allowances			22,313

Note. There is no restriction for private use where the asset is owned by a company.

Corporation tax computation

	£	£
Trading profits	50,000	
Less: CAs	(22,313)	
Schedule D Case I		27,687
Schedule D Case III		313
		28,000
Less: gift aid donation		(500)
PCTCT		27,500

Limits for starting rate marginal relief

£10,000 x 9/12 = £7,500

£50,000 x 9/12 = £37,500

Since the profits fall within the marginal rate relief band and a dividend has been paid to an individual during the period, the rules on non-corporate distributions apply.

Calculation of underlying rate

	£
£27,500 x 19%	5,225
Less: 19/400 x £(37,500 – 27,500)	(475)
	4,750

Underlying rate is:

$$\frac{4,750}{27,500} \times 100 \qquad\qquad 17.27272\%$$

CT Computation

	£
£10,000 x 19%	1,900
£(27,500 – 10,000) = £17,500 x 17.27272%	3,023
Total CT payable	4,923

7   PREPARATION QUESTION: LONG PERIOD OF ACCOUNT

> **Tutor's hint.** A long period of account must be split into two accounting periods. The first accounting period is always twelve months long. The rest of the period of account forms the second accounting period.

Corporation tax computations

	Accounting periods		
	12m to	*12m to*	*6m to*
	31.3.03	*31.3.04*	*30.9.04*
	£	£	£
Adjusted trading profits (p/e 30.9.04 12:6)	148,000	318,600	159,300
Less capital allowances (W1)	(65,250)	(81,971)	(11,500)
Schedule D Case I	82,750	236,629	147,800
Schedule D Case III	18,000	15,041	5,459
Chargeable gains	108,000	0	176,250
	208,750	251,670	329,509
Less charges paid	(3,750)	(3,750)	(1,500)
Profits chargeable to corporation tax	205,000	247,920	328,009
Dividends plus tax credits ($^{100}/_{90}$)	876	1,776	8,650
Profits for small companies rate purposes	205,876	249,696	336,659

	£	£	£
Corporation tax			
FY 2003 £205,000 × 19%	38,950		
FY 2003 £247,920 × 19%		47,105	
FY 2004 £328,009 × 30%			98,403
Less small companies marginal relief			
FY 2003 £(750,000 − 336,659) × $\frac{328,009}{336,659}$ × 11/400			(11,075)
Mainstream corporation tax	38,950	47,105	87,328
Due date	1.1.04	1.1.05	1.7.05

Note. As the company does not pay corporation tax at the full rate, payment of the tax is due nine months after the end of the accounting period rather than in quarterly instalments.

Workings

1   *Capital allowances*

	FYA £	Pool £	Expensive car £	Allowances £
Pool b/f		213,000		
12 months to 31.3.03				
Additions		36,000	16,500	
		249,000	16,500	
WDA at 25%		(62,250)	(3,000)	65,250
		186,750	13,500	
12 months to 31.3.04				
Additions		7,800		
Disposals		(70,000)		
		124,550	13,500	
WDA at 25%		(31,138)	(3,000)	34,138
		93,412	10,500	
Additions	119,583			
FYA at 40%	(47,833)			47,833
		71,750		81,971
6 months to 30.9.04				
Disposals		(3,994)		
		161,168	10,500	
WDA at 25% × 6/12		(20,146)	(1,313)	21,459
Additions	23,000			
FYA at 50%	(11,500)			11,500
		11,500		
		152,522	9,187	32,959

8   **UNFORESEEN ULTRASONICS LTD**

> **Tutor's hint.** You had to spot that the managing director's old car was cheap enough to have been pooled, even though his new car had to be kept out of that pool because it cost over £12,000.

Unforseen Ultrasonics Limited
Corporation tax computation

	£
Trading profit	2,300,000
Less capital allowances (W1)	(101,713)
Schedule D Case I	2,198,287
Less loss brought forward (no balance to c/f)	(600,000)
	1,598,287
Schedule D Case III £(1,500 + 80,000)	81,500
Chargeable gains (W2)	0
	1,679,787
Less charges	(5,000)
Profits chargeable to corporation tax	1,674,787

Corporation tax

The rates remain unchanged for FY03 and FY04 – thus £1,674,787 × 30% = £502,436

As Unforseen Ultrasonics Ltd pays corporation tax at the full rate, its corporation tax liability for the year to 31 December 2004 was due for payment by quarterly instalments as follows:

Due date	*Amount due*
	£
14 July 2004	125,609
14 October 2004	125,609
14 January 2005	125,609
14 April 2005	125,609
	502,436

Workings

1   *Capital allowances*

   (a)   The industrial building

   The total for the original building, excluding land, is £430,000, and the office part (£70,000) is less than 25% of this, so all £430,000 initially qualifies.

   The new extension (£60,000) puts the total cost of the office part up to £130,000, which is over 25% of the new total expenditure of £490,000: this means none of the expenditure on the offices will now qualify.

   IBAs are £360,000 × 4% = £14,400.

   (b)   Plant and machinery

	FYA	*Pool*	*Expensive car*	*Short-life asset*	*Total*
	£	£	£	£	£
WDV b/f		190,000		4,000	
Transfer		4,000		(4,000)	
		194,000			
Additions			18,000		
Disposals		(18,000)			
		176,000	18,000		
WDA @ 25%		(44,000)	(3,000)		47,000
Additions	80,625				
FYA @ 50%	(40,313)				40,313
		40,312			
					87,313
WDV c/f		172,312	15,000		

   As the company is a small enterprise, FYAs are due at 50%.

   (c)   Total allowances are £(14,400 + 87,312) = £101,712.

2 *Capital gains*

	£
Proceeds	72,493
Less: cost	(27,000)
Unindexed gain	45,493
Less: indexation allowance	
0.603 × £27,000	(16,281)
Indexed gain	29,212
Less: loss b/f	(29,212)
Chargeable gain	Nil
Loss c/f £(30,000 – 29,212)	£788

Marking guide

	Marks
Trading profit	1
Capital allowances	
- industrial building working	3
- plant and machinery working	4
Trade loss b/f	2
Sch D Case III	2
Gains	
- calculation	3
- offset of loss	1
- loss c/f	1
Gift aid payment	1
PCTCT	1
Corporation tax liability	3
Instalments of CT – amount due	2
Dates	2
	26

9 PLUG-IN-LTD

> **Tutor's hint**. This question is typical of the compulsory corporation tax question that appears in Section A of the exam. If you could answer this question well, you are well on your way towards passing the paper.

(a)

	£	£
Profits before tax		1,888,890
Add Increase in general bad debt provision	23,000	
Depreciation	93,770	
Gifts to customers (Food Hampers)	1,100	
Gift aid donation	750	
Legal fees	10,600	
Premium (W1)	60,000	
Entertaining	6,740	
		195,960
Less: Premium (W1)	2,880	
Bank interest	16,600	
IBAs (W2)	10,000	
Capital allowances	74,820	
		(104,300)
Schedule D Case I profits		1,980,550

Note 1. The **gifts to customers are allowable** as they bear a **conspicuous advertisement** for the business and they cost less than £50 each.

Note 2. As the **patent royalties relate to the trade**, they can be deducted **in computing Schedule D Case I profits**. The **deduction is made on an accruals basis** so no adjustment to accounts profit is needed.

Note 3. The costs of **entertaining staff and seconding employees to charity are allowable** expenses

(b)

	£
Schedule D Case I	1,980,550
Schedule D Case III	16,600
	1,997,150
Less: gift aid	(750)
PCTCT	1,996,400
CT @ 30%	£598,920

(c) (i) Plug-in Ltd is required to make quarterly payments of corporation tax, because it paid tax at the full rate in both the year to 31.12.04 and in the year to 31.12.03.

(ii) Quarterly payments were due as follows.

	£
14 July 2004	149,730
14 October 2004	149,730
14 January 2005	149,730
14 April 2005	149,730

Workings

1 *Premium*

The amount of the premium assessed under Schedule A on the landlord is:

	£
Premium	60,000
£60,000 × 2% × (15 – 1)	(16,800)
	43,200

Plug-in Ltd can deduct £2,880 per annum in computing its Schedule D Case I profits.

2 *Industrial buildings allowance*

Purchase price of factory (£440,000 – £130,000 – £95,000) £215,000

Original cost of factory (£486,500 - £145,000 - £105,000) £236,500

IBAs on lower, £215,000, over remaining tax life of 21½ years:

$$\frac{£215,000}{21.5} = £10,000 \text{ per annum}$$

£10,000 IBAs are available in the year to 31.12.04.

Note. IBAs are not available on the costs of offices as the cost of the offices exceeds 25 % of the total qualifying expenditure (including offices).

3   *Plant and machinery*

	FYA @ 40% £	General Pool £	SLA £	Allow-ances £
TWDV b/f		124,400	11,200	
Additions		10,200		
Disposals		(11,800)	(4,600)	
		122,800	6,600	
WDA x 25%		(30,700)		30,700
Balancing allowance			(6,600)	6,600
Addition	84,000			
FYA @ 40%	(33,600)			33,600
		50,400		
Addition	9,800			
FYA@40%	(3,920)			3,920
		5,880		
		148,380		74,820

Note. As Plug-In Ltd is a medium sized company for capital allowance purposes, FYA on the plant and machinery additions are available at 40% (not 50%)

Marking guide

		Marks
(a) Profit before tax		½
Depreciation		½
Bad debts		1
Gift to customers		2
Gift aid donation		1
Legal fees		1
Entertaining		1
Seconding employee to charity		1
Lease premium - Disallowance		1
- Deduction		1
Bank interest		½
Interest payable		1
Palent royalties		1
IBA	- Purchase price	1
	- General offices	1
	- 25-year life	1
	- WDA	1
P&M	- Pool	2
	- Short-life asset	1½
	- FYA	2
		22
(b) Schedule DI		1
Schedule DIII – Bank interest		1
Charges on income – gift aid donation		1
Corporation tax		1
		4
(c) *Quarterly instalment payments*		
Full tax rate for 2 years		2
Payment of corporation tax liability		
Instalments		1
Due dates		1
		4
		30

10 PREPARATION QUESTION: PLANT AND A FACTORY

> **Tutor's hint.** The tax benefit of capital allowances depends on the applicable rate of corporation tax, as set out in part (b). This fact may influence the timing of capital expenditure, if a company's tax rate fluctuates.
>
> As the company is a small enterprise for first year allowances purposes, 50% first year allowances are available. FYAs are not pro-rated in short periods.

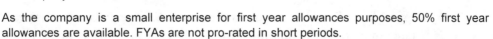

(a) **Capital allowances**

		£	Total £
(i)	*Computer equipment £2,500: FYA @ 50%*		1,250
(ii)	*Cars*		
	General pool: 25% × 10/12 × £5,000	1,042	
	Expensive: allowance restricted to £3,000 × 10/12	2,500	
			3,542
(iii)	*Plant £65,842 FYA @ 50%*		32,921

Industrial building

The original owner would have received IBAs but since the building was sold less than 25 years after 5 June 1990 a balancing charge would have been applied on sale. Freddie Ltd is given WDAs on the 'residue after sale' which is, generally, the lower of proceeds or original cost. Thus allowances will be given on £7,500 (£10,000 – £2,500). The building was 14 years 9 months old when Freddie acquired it. Of the 25 years tax life, 10 years 3 months (123 months) remain. Allowances of £7,500 × 12/123 are given each full year, but only 10/123 in this first, short period. Thus: £7,500 × 10/123

610

(iv)	*Extension to factory*		
	WDA 4% × 10/12 × £222,000		7,400
	Total allowances		45,723

(b) **The tax benefit of capital allowances**

For corporation tax purposes capital allowances are treated as a trading expense. They therefore reduce the taxable profit of the accounting period to which they relate. If Freddie Ltd makes profits exceeding £1,500,000 × 10/12 = £1,250,000, its profits will be taxed at 30%. The tax saved by virtue of the capital allowances will therefore be £45,723 × 30% = £13,717. If profits are less than £300,000 × 10/12 = £250,000 but above £50,000 × 10/12 = £41,667, the small companies rate of 19% will apply. The value of the allowances will then be £8,687. If profits are below £10,000 × 10/12 = £8,333, the starting rate of corporation tax applies and the value of allowances is then £NIL.

If profits fall between the limits of £1,250,000 and £250,000 the marginal rate of tax will be 32.75%, giving a tax saving of £14,974. If profits fall between the limits of £41,667 and £8,333, the marginal rate of tax will be 23.75% giving a tax saving of £10,859.

The cash flow benefit of the capital allowances will not be felt until the due date for payment of the mainstream corporation tax: provided the company does not pay tax at the full rate this will be 1 January 2006. If the company pays tax at the full rate it will normally have to make quarterly payments on account of its corporation tax liability.

If capital allowances create or increase a loss the benefit will be enjoyed only under the loss relief provisions. It would be beneficial to disclaim allowances so that profits were brought down to £8,333.

(c)   **Expenditure on office accommodation**

Rent payable is allowable as a trading expense. **A lease premium, to the extent that it is taxable income of the landlord, will be divided into yearly deductions depending on the length of the lease. No industrial buildings allowance is given on the purchase of office accommodation except for expenditure of not more than 25% of the cost of an industrial building.** Office equipment, including certain fixtures such as carpets, does attract capital allowances as plant. Repairs are deductible expenses unless disallowed as capital expenditure.

11   UNFORGETTABLE UNITS LIMITED

> **Tutor's hint.** It is very important that you learn to deal with industrial buildings allowances.

Corporation tax computation

	£
Schedule D Case I (W1)	756,465
Schedule D Case III (£64,000 + £5,000)	69,000
Less: charges on income paid	(58,000)
Profits chargeable to corporation tax	767,465

Corporation tax (W4)

	£
FY 2003 and FY 2004	
£767,465 × 30%	230,240
Less: 11/400 (1,500,000 – 779,965) × $\dfrac{767,465}{779,965}$	(19,484)
Corporation tax payable	210,756

Workings

1   *Schedule D Case I*

		£
Profit per accounts		822,875
Add:	Gift aid donations	58,000
	Fine	10,000
Less:	Reduction in bad debt provision	(5,000)
	Debenture interest	(64,000)
	Bank interest	(5,000)
	Dividend	(11,250)
	Capital allowances (W2)	(41,500)
	Industrial buildings allowance (W3)	(7,660)
Schedule D Case I		756,465

As fines are not incurred wholly and exclusively for the purpose of the trade they are not deductible in computing Schedule D Case I profits.

2   *Capital allowances*

	FYA £	Pool £	Expensive car £	Allow-ances £
TWDV b/f		100,000		
Addition			13,000	
Disposal		(2,000)		
		98,000	13,000	
WDA @ 25%/ restricted		(24,500)	(3,000)	27,500
Additions	35,000			
FYA @ 40%	(14,000)			14,000
		21,000		41,500
		94,500	10,000	

Unforgettable Units Ltd does not qualify for 50% first year allowances as it is not a small sized enterprise for capital allowance purposes.

3   *Industrial buildings allowance*

IBAs are due on the lower of purchase price (£150,000) and original cost (£250,000), ie on £150,000.

Tax life ends on 1.8.2023

Date of purchase is 1.1.2004

Unexpired life is therefore 19 years 7 months

Allowances due to Unforgettable Units Ltd

$$\frac{\text{Residue after sale}}{\text{Remaining tax life}} = \frac{150,000}{19\,^7/_{12}} = £7,660$$

4   *'Profits'*

	£
Profits chargeable to corporation tax	767,465
FII (£11,250 × 100/90)	12,500
'Profits'	779,965

As 'profits' are between the upper and lower limits for small companies' rate purposes for FY 2003 and FY 2004 small companies' marginal relief applies in both years.

12 PREPARATION QUESTION: CARRYING BACK A LOSS

> **Tutor's hint.** It was necessary to spot that starting rate marginal relief would apply in the year to 31 March 2005.

(a)

	Year ended 31 March		
	2003	2004	2005
	£	£	£
Schedule D Case I	125,000	0	50,000
Less s 393(1) loss relief	0	0	(6,640)
	125,000	0	43,360
Schedule D Case III	263,000	10,000	24,000
Chargeable gains (loss c/f)	60,360	0	0
	448,360	10,000	67,360
Less s 393A(1) current loss relief	0	(10,000)	0
	448,360	0	67,360
Less: s 393A carry back	(448,360)	0	0
Less: gift aid donation	0	0	(30,000)
Profits chargeable to corporation tax	0	0	37,360
Unrelieved gift aid donation	40,000	47,000	0

The loss carried back is £465,000 – £10,000 = £455,000. The loss remaining to carry forward is £455,000 - £448,360 = £6,640.

There is no corporation tax liability for either of the first two years.

For the third year, the position is as follows.

Profits chargeable to corporation tax = £37,360

'Profits' = £37,360 + (£3,750 × 100/90) = £41,527. As 'profits' are between the starting rate upper and lower limits of £50,000 and £10,000 respectively, starting rate marginal relief applies.

	£
Corporation tax	
£37,360 × 19%	7,098
Less: starting rate marginal relief	
$^{19}/_{400}$ (£50,000 − £41,527) × $\dfrac{37,360}{41,527}$	(362)
	6,736

The current year set off is, in some ways, not worth taking in this question as the company's profits **would otherwise be largely covered by the gift aid donation.** However, if a current year set off is not made a s 393A carryback claim cannot be made. In this case carrying the loss back saves tax at 32.75%, 19% and 23.75% and 0%. The claim must be for the whole of the loss under s393A. If s 393A claims were not made the loss would have to be carried forward and, based on current year profits, relief would be at 23.75%, 19% and 0% in future years. Full relief would not be available for several years.

(b) The due date for payment of the £6,736 corporation tax for the year to 31 March 2005 is 1 January 2006. The filing date is 31 March 2006. **Galbraith Ltd is not required to pay its anticipated corporation tax liability in quarterly instalments as it does not pay corporation tax at the full rate.**

13 LOSER LTD

> **Tutor's hint**. In a question where there is more than one loss always deal with the losses in chronological order.

(a) A company's choice of loss relief will be influenced by:

(i) the **tax rate at which relief will be obtained**. Preferably, losses should be relieved at the small companies' marginal rate of 32.75%.

(ii) the **timing of relief**. Earlier relief is better than later relief.

(iii) the **extent to which gift aid donations become unrelieved**.

(b)

	Year to 30.6.02	p/e 31.3.03	y/e 31.3.04	y/e 31.3.05
	£	£	£	£
Schedule D Case I	98,400	-	43,700	-
Schedule A		4,500	8,100	5,600
	98,400	4,500	51,800	
Less: Schedule A loss	(3,600)			
Less: s 393A current		(4,500)		(5,600)
Less: s 393A c/b	(21,200)		(51,800)	
	73,600	-	-	-
Less: gift aid	(1,400)			
PCTCT	72,200	-	-	-
Unrelieved gift aid		£800	£1,200	£1,100

Loss memorandum

	£
Loss p/e 31.3.03	25,700
S 393A current	(4,500)
	21,200
Less: s 393A c/b	(21,200)

	£
Loss y/e 31.3.05	78,300
S 393A current	(5,600)
S 393A c/b	(51,800)
Loss remaining to c/f at 1.4.05	20,900

(c) If Loser Ltd had ceased trading, the loss in the final period could be carried back to set against total profits in the previous 36 months. This means that a loss of £20,900 would have been relieved in the year ended 30.6.02 reducing PCTCT to £51,300.

Marking guide

		Marks
(a)	Tax rate	1
	Timing	1
	Gift aid	1
		3
(b)	Schedule DI	1
	Schedule A	1
	Schedule A loss	2
	S 393A current	2
	S 393A c/b	2
	Gift aid	2
		10
(c)	36 months	1
	All loss relieved	1
		2
		15

14   PREPARATION QUESTION: A BUILDING AND SHARES

Tutor's hint. Rollover relief is not automatically available on the facts given: conditions relating to trade use and the time of acquisition must be satisfied.

(a) (i)   **The building**

	£
Proceeds	200,000
Less cost	(65,000)
Unindexed gain	135,000
Less indexation allowance £65,000 × 0.893	(58,045)
Chargeable gain	76,955

(ii)   **The Z plc shares**

	Shares	Cost £	Indexed cost £
The FA 1985 pool			
May 1983 acquisition	2,000	4,000	4,000
Indexation to April 1985:			
£4,000 × 0.065			260
			4,260
Indexed rise to March 1987:			
£4,260 × 0.061			260
March 1987 acquisition	2,000	5,000	5,000
	4,000	9,000	9,520
Indexed rise to July 2004:			
£9,520 × 0.837			7,968
			17,488
July 2004 disposal	(4,000)	(9,000)	(17,488)
	0	0	0

	£
Sale proceeds	22,000
Less cost	(9,000)
	13,000
Less indexation allowance £(17,488 – 9,000)	(8,488)
Indexed gain	4,512

Total chargeable gains for the year are £76,955 + £4,512 = £81,467.

Corporation tax payable thereon is £81,467 × 30% = £24,440.

(b)   **If the non-industrial building was occupied and used for trading purposes and the sale proceeds are reinvested in another building (or other qualifying asset) for use in the company's trade, within 12 months before or 36 months after the disposal, capital gains rollover relief will be available.**

If the new qualifying building costs £225,000, full rollover relief will be available with the chargeable gain arising on the disposal (£76,955) being deducted from the acquisition cost of the new building, to give the revised base cost of that asset.

When not all of the sale proceeds of a qualifying asset are reinvested, the gain which becomes immediately chargeable is the lower of:

(i)   the gain on disposal of the old asset; and
(ii)   the proceeds not reinvested in the new asset.

Thus, if the new building costs £175,000, a gain of £25,000 becomes chargeable immediately, with the balance of £76,955 – £25,000 = £51,955 being rolled over.

15   ASTUTE LTD

> **Tutor's hint.** When this question was set the examiner said there was little awareness of the reinvestment period and that the reinvestment in the depreciating asset caused problems.

(a)   For rollover relief to be available:

(i)   A new asset must be acquired **in the period commencing 12 months before and ending 3 years after the disposal.**

(ii)   Both **the old and the new assets must be used for trade purposes and must be on the list of qualifying assets.**

(iii)   The new asset must **immediately be brought into trade use.**

(b)

	£
Disposal proceeds	320,000
Less: Cost	(164,000)
Legal fees on purchase	(3,600)
Extension	(37,000)
Legal fees on sale	(6,200)
Gain	109,200
Less: Indexation	
(£164,000 + 3,600) × 0.132	(22,123)
£37,000 × 0.106	(3,922)
Chargeable gain	83,155

Note 1

Enhancement expenditure reflected in the state or nature of an asset at the date of disposal can be deducted in computing a chargeable gain.

The factory extension is enhancement expenditure as it has added to the value of the factory.

The replacement of the roof is a repair, not enhancement expenditure, so the cost is not deductible.

(c)   (i)   Purchase of a warehouse.
All proceeds are reinvested.
∴ gain rolled over – £83,155
Base cost of warehouse
£340,000 – £83,155 = £256,845

(ii)   Freehold office building £275,000
Proceeds not reinvested = £45,000
Gain rolled over =
£83,155 – £45,000 = £38,155
Base cost of building
£275,000 – £38,155 = £236,845

(iii)   Leasehold Factory
Proceeds fully reinvested
∴ Gain deferred = £83,155

The factory is a depreciating asset. This means that the base cost of the factory is not adjusted. It is £350,000. The gain is merely deferred until the earliest of 10 years from the date of acquisition or the date the leasehold factory is disposed of or the date it ceases to be used in the trade.

Marking guide

		Marks
	Rollover relief period	
(a)	Period of reinvestment	1
	Old/new assets used for trade	1
	Brought into business use	1
		3
(b)	Net sale proceeds	1
	Deductions	2
	Indexation on cost/enhancement	2
		5
(c)	Freehold warehouse	
	Full Rollover relief	1
	Base cost	1
	Freehold office building	
	Amount not rolled over	1
	Base cost	1
	Leasehold factory	
	Gain deferral	1
	Depreciating asset	1
	10 years/date of sale/not used in trade	1
		7
		15

16   EAGLE LTD

> **Tutor's hint.** You needed to remember that a s 393A ICTA 1988 claim can only be made to carry a loss back against profits of the previous 12 months.

(a) **Schedule D Case I trading loss**

	£
Trading loss	(259,900)
Less: Patent royalties payable	(20,000)
Industrial buildings allowances (W1)	(7,600)
Capital allowances (W2)	(32,500)
Schedule D Case I trading loss	320,000

(b)

		y/e 30.9.03 £	6 m/e 31.3.04 £	y/e 31.3.05 £
	Schedule D Case I	152,100	65,700	-
	Schedule A (W3)	-	18,700	49,950
	Chargeable gain (W4)	-	9,300	22,932
			93,700	72,882
Less:	Schedule A loss	(4,600)		
		147,500		
Less:	S 393A current			(72,882)
	S 393A c/b	(73,750)	(93,700)	
		73,750	-	-
Less:	gift aid donation	(2,300)		
	PCTCT	71,450	-	-

Loss memorandum

		£
Loss		320,000
Less:	S 393A current	(72,882)
	S 393A c/b	(93,700)
	S 393A c/b (6/12 × £147,500)	(73,750)
Loss c/f		79,668

Note. The gift aid donations in the 6 months to 31.3.04 and the year to 31.3.05 cannot be carried forward. They remain unrelieved.

(c) As an alternative to making s 393A claims in both the current year and previous periods, the company could:

(i) make no s 393A claims and carry the whole of the loss forward

(ii) make a current year s 393A ICTA 1988 claim and then carry the balance of the loss forward.

Workings

1 *Industrial buildings allowances*

	£
Factory	141,000
Canteen	32,000
Site preparation	12,000
Architect's fees	5,000
	190,000

Note. The cost of the general offices does not qualify as it exceeds 25% of the total cost.

IBAS @ 4% = £7,600

2 *Capital allowances*

	FYA £	General pool £	Expensive motor car £	Allow- ances £
TWDV b/f		64,700	14,700	
Disposals			(12,400)	
Addition		11,300		
		76,000	2,300	
WDA @ 25%		(19,000)		19,000
Balancing allowance			(2,300)	2,300
Addition	22,400			
FYA @ 50%	(11,200)	11,200		11,200
		68,200		32,500

Note. As Eagle Ltd is a small enterprise for capital allowance purposes, FYA are available at 50% on expenditure in the one year commencing 1 April 2004.

3 *Schedule A*

	£
Warehouse 1	
Premium (£50,000 – 2% × £50,000 × 7)	43,000
Rent (£12,600 × 9/12)	9,450
Warehouse 2	
Rent (£8,400 × 9/12)	6,300
Bad debt	(2,100)
Repairs to roof	(6,700)
	49,950

4   *Capital gain*

	£
Proceeds	156,000
Less: cost	(112,800)
	43,200
Less: indexation	(20,268)
	22,932

Note. Companies are entitled to indexation until the date of disposal of an asset.

The capital loss of £8,900 in the year ended 30.9.03 is carried forward and offset against the £18,200 gain in the 6 month period to 31.3.04 leaving a gain of £9,300 chargeable.

Marking scheme

		Marks
(a)	*IBAs*	
	Qualifying expenditure	1
	Offices not qualifying	1
	4% allowance	1
	Land not qualifying	1
	CAs:	
	Expensive car	1
	Addition to pool	1
	25% WDA	1
	50% FYA	1
	Schedule D I loss	
	Patent royalties	2
		10
(b)	Schedule D Case I	1
	Schedule A: warehouse 1	3
	warehouse 2	3
	Chargeable gain: y/e 30.3.05	1
	p/e 30.3.04	1
	Schedule A loss relief	2
	S 393A current	1
	c/b p/e 31.3.04	1
	c/b y/e 30.9.03	2
	Gift aid donations	1
	Amount c/f	1
		17
(c)	No s 393A ICTA 1988 claims	1½
	Current year s 393A ICTA 1988 claim only	1½
		3
		30

17 PREPARATION QUESTION: FOREIGN TAX

> **Tutor's hint.** The four associated companies reduce Mumbo Ltd's upper limit for small companies' marginal relief purposes to £300,000 and this makes marginal relief unavailable. This greatly simplifies the calculation.

Mumbo Ltd
Corporation tax computation

	£	£
Schedule D Case I		550,000
Schedule D Case V		
Z Inc: £36,000 × 100/72	50,000	
X SA: £38,000 × 100/95	40,000	
		90,000
		640,000
Less charge paid		(60,000)
Profits chargeable to corporation tax		580,000

	£
Corporation tax £580,000 × 30%	174,000
Less double taxation relief (W)	(16,000)
Mainstream corporation tax	158,000

Working: double taxation relief

Neither foreign tax rate exceeds the UK corporation tax rate, and the charges can all be set against UK profits. Full relief is therefore available for foreign tax.

	Profits	*Charges*	*Net profits*	*Corporation tax at 30%*	*DTR*
	£	£	£	£	£
UK	550,000	60,000	490,000	147,000	0
Z Inc	50,000	0	50,000	15,000	14,000
X SA	40,000	0	40,000	12,000	2,000
Total	640,000	60,000	580,000	174,000	16,000

18 B AND W LTD

> **Tutor's hint.** The set off of DTR must be made on a source by source basis.

Mainstream corporation tax

	B Ltd	*W Ltd*
	£	£
Schedule D Case I	296,000	6,000
Capital gains	30,000	0
Schedule D Case V (× 100/80)	2,000	0
Schedule D Case III	8,000	0
Less charge on income	(18,000)	0
PCTCT	318,000	6,000
FII	32,000	0
'Profits'	350,000	6,000

B Ltd
FY03 & FY04

Lower limit for small companies rate	£150,000
Upper limit for small companies rate	£750,000

Small companies' marginal relief applies.

	£
£318,000 × 30%	95,400
Less: $^{11}/_{400}$ (750,000 – 350,000) × $\frac{318,000}{350,000}$	(9,994)
	85,406
Less DTR (W1)	(400)
Mainstream corporation tax	85,006

W Ltd

CT	£
FY 2003 & FY2004	
£6,000 × 19%	1,140
Less: starting rate marginal relief (W2)	
19/400 (£25,000 £6,000)	(903)
Mainstream corporation tax	237

Workings

1   *Double tax relief*

	UK profits £	Schedule D Case V £	Total £
Profits	334,000	2,000	336,000
Less: charges	(18,000)	–	(18,000)
	316,000	2,000	318,000
CT $\frac{85,406}{318,000}$ = 26.85723%			
	84,869	537	85,406
Less: DTR			
lower of			
(i) UK tax (£537)			
(ii) Overseas tax (£400)		(400)	(400)
	84,869	137	85,006

2   *CT*

The upper and lower limits for starting rate purposes are £25,000 and £5,000 respectively so starting rate marginal relief applies.

Marking guide

		Marks
B Ltd -	Schedule DI	½
	Capital gains	½
	Schedule DV	1
	Schedule DIII	½
	Charge on income	1
	FII	1
W Ltd -	Schedule DI/PCTCT	½
B Ltd -	FY03 & FY04 Tax calculation	3
DTR -	UK profits	1
	Schedule DV	1
	Average rate of CT	1
	DTR set off	1
W Ltd -	CT	3
		15

19   WASH PLC

> **Tutor's hint**. All the topics covered in this question were covered in an examiner's article in *Student Accountant*. This highlights the importance of reading articles in *Student Accountant*. Such articles can be accessed on the ACCA's website: accaglobal.com.

(a)   **Withholding tax is overseas tax that is deducted at source from an overseas dividend. Relief for withholding tax is always available.**

Underlying tax is the overseas tax that has been paid by the overseas subsidiary on the profits out of which the overseas dividend is paid. **Relief** for underlying tax **is available** if the UK company receiving the dividend **holds at least 10% of the voting power** of the overseas subsidiary.

(b)   **Wash plc: y/e 31.3.05**

	£
Schedule D Case I	1,600,000
Schedule D Case V (W1)	420,000
	2,020,000

	£
CT @ 30% =	606,000
Less: DTR (W2)	(126,000)
Corporation tax	480,000

(c)   The **transfer pricing legislation** applies to sales made at an undervalue by Wash Ltd to Dry Inc. This legislation requires Wash plc to adjust the selling price of the goods to their market value in its corporation tax self assessment return. The market value is the price that the goods would fetch if sold to an independent party in an arm's length trans action. **The adjustment will increase the profits of Wash plc.**

Workings

1   *Schedule D Case V*

	£
Dividend paid + w/h tax	300,000
Underlying tax: $\dfrac{£300,000}{420,000} \times £168,000$	120,000
Schedule D Case V	420,000

2   *Double tax relief*

DTR is the lower of

(i)	UK tax (£420,000 × 30%)	£126,000
(ii)	Overseas tax (£120,000 + £30,000)	£150,000

Marking guide			Marks
(a)	Withholding tax	- description	1
		- always get relief	1
	Underlying tax	- description	1
		- 10% of votes	1
			4
(b)	Schedule DI		1
	Schedule DV		1
	Underlying tax		2
	Total overseas tax		1
	Double taxation relief		1
	Corporation tax		1
			7
(c)	Transfer pricing legislation applies		1
	Sale at market value		1
	Definition of market value		1
	Adjustment under self assessment		1
			4
			15

20 PREPARATION QUESTION: GROUP RELIEF

> **Tutor's hint.** You are asked to use group relief in the most efficient manner. This means giving it first to companies in the small companies' marginal relief band, then to companies paying tax at the full rate and then to companies in the starting rate marginal relief band. You must recognise that T Ltd is an associated company, being under common control with the P Ltd group.

(a) There are six associated companies, so the lower and upper limits for small companies' rate purposes are £50,000 and £250,000 respectively. The upper and lower limits for starting rate purposes are £8,333 and £1,667 respectively.

S Ltd and T Ltd are outside the P Ltd group for group relief purposes. P Ltd's loss should be surrendered first to Q Ltd, to bring its taxable profits down to £50,000, then to R Ltd to bring its taxable profits down to £50,000 and finally to M Ltd.

Note that there is no point in P Ltd setting off any of its own loss as P Ltd is not subject to tax on its PCTCT.

	M Ltd £	P Ltd £	Q Ltd £	R Ltd £	S Ltd £	T Ltd £
Schedule D Case I	10,000	0	64,000	260,000	0	70,000
Schedule A	0	6,000	4,000	0	0	0
	10,000	6,000	68,000	260,000	0	70,000
Less charges	(4,000)	(4,500)	(2,000)	(5,000)	0	0
	6,000	1,500	66,000	255,000	0	70,000
Less group relief	(2,000)	0	(16,000)	(205,000)	0	0
PCTCT	4,000	1,500	50,000	50,000	0	70,000
Corporation tax: at 0%		0				
at 19%	760		9,500	9,500	0	
at 30%						21,000
Less starting rate marginal relief						
19/400 × £(8,333 – 4,000)	(206)					
Less: small companies rate marginal relief						
11/400 (£250,000–70,000)						(4,950)
MCT payable	554	0	9,500	9,500	0	16,050

(b) If P Ltd were to acquire another 8% of the share capital of S Ltd, bringing the total holding to 75%, S Ltd's losses could be surrendered to P Ltd, Q Ltd, R Ltd or M Ltd.

21 PREPARATION QUESTION: CORRESPONDING ACCOUNTING PERIODS

> **Tutor's hint.** The maximum group relief in each corresponding period is the lower of the time-apportioned profits and the time-apportioned losses.

Harry Ltd

	12 months to 31.12.03	9 months to 30.9.04
	£	£
Schedule D Case I	25,000	0
Schedule A	3,000	4,000
	28,000	4,000
Less charges on income	(2,000)	(2,000)
Profits chargeable to corporation tax	26,000	2,000
Corporation tax payable		
£26,000 × 19%	4,940	
£2,000 × 0%		0
Mainstream corporation tax	4,940	0

Sid Ltd

	12 months to 31.3.04	12 months to 31.3.05
	£	£
Schedule D Case I	52,000	250,000
Schedule D Case III	8,000	10,000
	60,000	260,000
Less charges on income	(5,000)	(5,000)
	55,000	255,000
Less group relief (W)	(13,750)	(30,000)
Profits chargeable to corporation tax	41,250	225,000

Corporation tax payable

	£	£
FY 2003		
£41,250 × 19%	7,838	
FY 2004		
£225,000 × 30%		67,500
Less small companies marginal relief		
Less 11/400 × (750,000 – 225,000)		(14,438)
Mainstream corporation tax	7,838	53,062

Working: group relief

	£
Loss in 9 month accounting period to 30.9.04	45,000
Less surrender to Sid Ltd (y/e 31.3.04), restricted to lower of:	
(i) £45,000 × 3/9 = £15,000	
(ii) £55,000 × 3/12 = £13,750	(13,750)
	31,250
Less surrender to Sid Ltd (y/e 31.3.05), restricted to lower of:	
(i) £45,000 × 6/9 = £30,000	(30,000)
(ii) £255,000 × 6/12 = £127,500	
Unrelieved loss carried forward	1,250

22   **APPLE LTD**

> **Tutor's hint.** The marginal rate of tax of 32.75% is an effective tax rate only. It is never actually used in working out corporation tax.

(a)   Group relief is available within a 75% group. This is one where one company is a 75% subsidiary of another company or both are 75% subsidiaries of a third company. The holding company must have at least 75% of the ordinary share capital of the subsidiary; a right to at least 75% of the distributable income of the subsidiary; and the right to at least 75% of the net assets of the subsidiary were it to be wound up.

Two companies are in a group only if there is a 75% effective interest eg if Company A holds 90% of Company B which holds 90% of Company C, all three companies are in a group because 90% × 90% = 81%.

(b)   Group relief should be allocated to the company with the highest marginal rate of tax. This is Cherry Ltd and Apple Ltd to the extent that profits exceed £100,000 since the small companies rate lower limit is £300,000 ÷ 3 = £100,000. Such profits are taxed at the marginal rate of 32.75%. Then, the remainder of the loss should be set against the profits of Banana Ltd which bears tax at 30%. The capital loss cannot be group relieved.

(c)   Rollover relief for part of Apple Ltd's gain can be claimed in respect of the investment by Cherry Ltd. The excess of amount of proceeds over the amount invested remains in charge ie £(418,000 – 290,000) = £128,000.

An election should be made so that the asset disposed of at a loss by Banana Ltd is treated as having been disposed of by Apple Ltd. Apple Ltd will then be able to offset the loss of £8,000 against the gain of £128,000, leaving £120,000 chargeable.

Apple Ltd should then make a current year loss relief claim to bring its profits down to £100,000.

	Apple Ltd £	*Banana Ltd* £	*Cherry Ltd* £
Schedule DI	-	650,000	130,000
Net Capital gain	120,000	-	-
	120,000	650,000	130,000
Less: s 393A(1)	(20,000)		
group relief		(75,000)	(30,000)
PCTCT	100,000	575,000	100,000
Tax @ 19%	19,000		19,000
Tax @ 30%		172,500	

Note that the SCR upper limit is £1,500,000 ÷ 3 = £500,000.

23   ALPHABETIC LTD

> **Tutor's hint.** This question includes self assessment and the payment of corporation tax by quarterly instalments. These areas are extremely topical.

(a) Alphabetic Ltd is a 'large' company and as such should have paid its corporation tax liability for the year to 30 September 2004 in four quarterly instalments. The underpayments were:

Due date	Amount Due £	Underpaid £
14.4.04	200,000	44,000
14.7.04	200,000	44,000
14.10.04	200,000	44,000
14.1.05	200,000	44,000

Interest will run on each of the amounts of £44,000 underpaid from the due date until the date of payment, 1 July 2005.

(b) **If a company has not received a return it must notify the Revenue of its liability to corporation tax within 12 months of the end of its accounting period.**

The maximum penalty for not taking such action is 100% of the corporation tax unpaid twelve months after the end of the accounting period.

(c) (i) **Fixed rate penalties**

(1) **Where the return is up to 3 months late - £100**

(2) **Where the return is more than 3 months late - £200**

(3) **Where the return is the third consecutive one to be filed late the above penalties are increased to £500 and £1,000 respectively.**

(ii) **A tax geared penalty is triggered in addition to the fixed penalties if a return is more than six months late. The penalty is 10% of any tax unpaid six months after the return was due if the total delay is up to 12 months, but 20% of that tax if the return is over 12 months late.**

(d) **Companies that become large during an accounting period will not have to pay their corporation tax for that period by instalments if:**

(i) **their taxable profits for the period do not exceed £10 million** (reduced if there are associated companies); and

(ii) **they were not a large company in the previous period**

A 'large company' is one that pays corporation tax at the full rate.

Also, there is a de minimis limit in that any company whose liability does not exceed £10,000 need not pay by instalments.

Marking guide

			Marks
(a)	Quarterly instalments		
	– due date		1
	– amount due		1
	– amount underpaid		1
	Interest position		1
			4
(b)	Notification within 12 months		1
	Penalty		1
			2
(c) (i)	Fixed rate penalty	- up to 3 months	1
		- more than 3 months	1
		- consecutive late filing	2
			4
(ii)	Tax geared penalty	- when applicable	1
		- amounts	2
			3
(d) (i)	Companies becoming large		1
(ii)	De minimis limit		1
			2
			15

24 PREPARATION QUESTION: COMPUTING VAT DUE

> **Tutor's hint.** VAT is due on the discounted amount whether or not the settlement discount is taken up. Bad debt relief is available if at least six months have elapsed since the payment of a debt was due.

	£	£
Output VAT		
£(210,000 - 20,000) × 17.5%		33,250
£20,000 × 0.95 × 17.5%		3,325
		36,575
Input VAT		
£130,000 × 17.5%	22,750	
Bad debt relief £4,000 × 17.5%	700	
		(23,450)
VAT due		13,125

25 NEWCOMER LTD, ONGOING LTD AND AU REVOIR LTD

> **Tutor's hint.**
>
> 1 Where a discount is offered for prompt payment, VAT is chargeable on the net amount, regardless of whether the discount is taken up.
>
> 2 VAT on business entertaining is not recoverable where the cost of the entertaining is not a deductible Schedule D Case I expense.
>
> 3 Bad debt relief is only available for debts over six months old (measured from when the payment is due).
>
> 4 VAT incurred on the purchase of a car not used wholly for business purposes is not recoverable.

(a) The registration threshold is £58,000 (from 1.4.04) during any 12 month consecutive period.

This is exceeded in January 2005:

		£
2004	October	11,500
	November	14,200
	December	21,400
2005	January	12,300
		59,400

Therefore, Newcomer Ltd must register within 30 days of the end of the period ie by 2 March 2005.

Newcomer Ltd will be registered from 1 March 2005 or an earlier date agreed between the company and Customs.

(b)

	£	£
Output tax		
£120,000 × 95% = 114,000 × 17.5%		19,950
Input tax		
£(35,640 – 480) = 35,160 × 17.5%	6,153	
£2,000 × 17.5%	350	
£21,150 × 7/47	3,150	(9,653)
VAT payable		10,297

(c) A person is eligible for voluntary deregistration if Customs are satisfied that the rate of his taxable supplies (net of VAT) in the following one year period will not exceed £56,000 (from 1.4.04). However, voluntary deregistration will not be allowed if the reasons for the expected fall in value of taxable supplies is the cessation of taxable supplies or the suspension of taxable supplies for a period of 30 days or more in that following year. Customs will cancel a person's registration from the date the request is made or an agreed later date.

26   SELF ASSESSMENT FOR INDIVIDUALS

> **Tutor's hint.** It was important to confine your answer to the points asked for in the question.

(a) (i)   **The later of 30 September following the tax year to which the return relates and 2 months after the notice to file the return was issued.**

    (ii) **The later of 31 January following the tax year to which the return relates and 3 months after notice to file the return was issued.**

(b) (i)   The normal payment dates for Schedule D Case I and II income tax are:

- **31 January in the tax year for the first payment on account,** ie 31.1.05
- **31 July following the tax year for the second payment on account,** ie 31.7.05
- **31 January following the tax year for the final payment,** ie 31.1.06

    (ii) **Each of the payments on account is normally equal to half of the Schedule D Case I or II liability for the preceding year,** (in this case 2003/04).

The **final payment is the balancing payment.** It is the difference between the tax which is finally due for 2004/05 and the payments on account which have already been made in respect of the year.

(c) **Payments on account are not required if the relevant amount falls below £500.**

      Also, payments on account are not required from taxpayers who paid 80% or more of their tax liability for the previous year under PAYE or other deduction at source arrangements.

(d) (i) The **fixed penalty** for not making a tax return by the filing date (31 January following the tax year) when required to do so is initially **£100**. If the **delay is more than six months** from the filing date, and the Revenue did not apply for a daily penalty within those six months, there is a **further £100 fixed penalty**.

      (ii) The total of the £100 fixed penalties is reduced to the amount of the final payment of tax, if that is less than that total. The commissioners can set aside the fixed £100 penalties if they find that the taxpayer had a reasonable excuse for his conduct.

      (iii) Where the Revenue are of the opinion that the fixed penalties imposed will not result in the return being submitted they may ask the Commissioners to apply further penalties of up to £60 a day until the return is submitted.

Marking guide			
			Marks
(a)	(i)	30 September/2 months after notice	2
	(ii)	31 January/3 months after notice	2
			4
(b)	(i)	31.1.05	1
		31.7.05	1
		31.1.06	1
	(ii)	Payments on account - ½ preceding year	1
		Final payment - balance	1
			5
(c)		£500/80% limit	2
(d)	(i)	No return by filing date - £100	1
		More than 6 months late – further £100	1
	(ii)	Reduction penalty if less than £100	1
	(iii)	Daily penalty	1
			4
			15

27 ENQUIRIES AND DETERMINATIONS

> **Tutor's hint.** Do not select a question like this unless you are sure that you can give a concise answer to all parts.

(a) **The Revenue must normally give notice of an enquiry by the first anniversary of the due filing date (not the actual filing date).**

(b) **If a return is filed late, the deadline by which the Revenue must give notice of an enquiry is extended to 12 months after the 31 January, 30 April, 31 July or 31 October next following the actual date of delivery of the return or amendment.**

(c) **The three main reasons** why the Revenue commence enquiries into a return are:

      (i) **random selection** of the return

      (ii) **the return appears unusual**; there appears to be either an underdeclaration or income or allowances appear to have been incorrectly claimed

      (iii) **the Revenue suspect or have been informed of irregularities** in the return

(d) Once the enquiry is complete the Revenue will issue a closure notice indicating that each aspect of the enquiry is completed. The Inspector will also make any amendments to the taxpayer's self assessment return which he considers are necessary. The taxpayer has 20 days from the issue of the closure notice to appeal against the Inspector's findings.

(e) A determination is an assessment of the amounts liable to income tax and CGT and the amount of tax due. It is issued by the Revenue where the taxpayer has not submitted a return by the due filing date. It is treated as a self assessment.

A determination must be made by the 5th anniversary of 31 January following the end of the tax year.

Marking Guide

			Marks
(a)	Anniversary of due filing date		1
(b)	Return filed late	1	
	12 months after end of relevant quarter	4	
			5
(c)	(i) Random	1	
	(ii) Return unusual	1	
	(iii) Suspect irregularities	1	
			3
(d)	Closure notice	½	
	Revenue make amendments	½	
	30 days to appeal	1	
			2
(e)	IT/CGT and tax	1	
	No return	1	
	Self assessment	1	
	Time limit	1	
			4
			15

28   MADELAINE AND OTTO

Tutor's hint. It was important to state why any additional information is needed as well as what information is required.

(a)

	Additional information needed	Reasons
1	Sales	
	Were any goods taken for own use?	The market value must be included in sales
2	Stock	
	Were any contingency reserves included in the stock valuations?	These should be added back when calculating Schedule D Case I profits.
3	Wages and National Insurance contributions	
	(a) Were Madelaine's NIC contributions included?	If so they should be disallowed.
	(b) Were any payments made to Madelaine?	If so they should be disallowed.

Additional information needed	Reasons
(c) Were any payments made to Madelaine's family?	Payments should be reasonable for the work done. Excessive payments should be disallowed.
4 Repairs and Renewals	
Was any capital expenditure included?	If so it should be disallowed.
5 General expenses	
Were any of these of a non-trading or capital nature?	If so they will be disallowed.
6 Bad debts	
Were there any specific or general provisions made?	Only specific provisions are allowable.
7 Interest	
Did the charge include any interest on overdue tax?	If so it should be disallowed.
8 Relocation expenditure	
Was the move to larger premises?	If so the expenditure will be disallowed.
9 Professional fees	
Did these include any costs in connection with capital items?	If so they will be disallowed.
10 (a) Rent and rates	
(b) Interest	
(c) Motor vehicle running costs	
(d) Lighting and heating	
(e) Professional fees	
(f) Subscriptions and donations	
Was there any private element in any of the above items?	If so, it should be disallowed.
11 Subscriptions and donations	
Were the donations made wholly and exclusively for trade purposes?	If not they will be disallowed.
What did the subscriptions relate to?	To be allowable they must either be wholly and exclusively for trade purposes or to a body on the Revenue approved list.

BPP
PROFESSIONAL EDUCATION

(b)   £

2001/02 (1.6.01 – 5.4.02)

£7,000 + 4/12 × £16,000   12,333

2002/03 (1.12.01 – 30.11.02)   16,000

2003/04 (1.12.02 – 30.11.03)   19,000

Overlap profits on commencement were £16,000 × 4/12 = £5,333. The overlap period was 4 months long.

                                                                                       £

2004/05 (1.12.03 - 28.2.05)   25,000

Less: Overlap relief 3/4 × £5,333   (4,000)

Taxable   21,000

In 2004/05, 3 months worth of the overlap profits are relieved. **This ensures that only 12 months worth of profits are taxed in the year**.

Marking guide

		Marks
(a)	Goods taken for own use	$1/2$
	Contingency reserves	$1/2$
	Wages and NICs	1
	Payments to family	$1/2$
	Repairs/renewals	$1/2$
	General expenses	1
	Bad debts	1
	Interest	$1/2$
	Relocation expenditure	1
	Professional fees	$1/2$
	Private usage	1
	Subscriptions and donations	1
		9
(b)	2001/02	2
	2002/03 and 2003/04	1
	2004/05 15 months less overlap	3
		6
		15

---

29   MALCOLM

Tutor's hint. You should not be tempted in a question like this merely to list the various loss sections. You need to make an attempt at giving your rationale for the use of the losses. Remember that you will probably get marks for your rationale even if you have not used the loss in the most efficient way.

(a)   Schedule D Case I losses are:

	£	£
2003/04 (1.8.03 - 5.4.04)		
(£10,000 + 4/12 × £20,000)		(16,667)
2004/05 (1.12.03 - 30.11.04)		
Loss	20,000	
Less: Used in 2003/04	(6,667)	
		(13,333)

Each of these losses can be relieved under s 380 ICTA 1988 against STI of the year of the loss and/or the preceding year.

2003/04 loss

	2002/03 £	2003/04 £
Employment income	8,000	5,650
Interest	3,800	3,800
STI	11,800	9,450
S 380 loss relief	(11,800)	(4,867)
	0	4,583

A s 380 ICTA 1988 claim in 2002/03 results in a waste of personal allowances. However, the claim is worthwhile as it leads to a repayment of income tax in respect of the year and the alternative is to carry the loss forward.

A s 380 ICTA 1988 claim in 2003/04 to utilise the balance of the 2003/04 loss obtains tax relief for the loss quickly and it only wastes a small amount of personal allowance.

2004/05 loss

A s380 claim in 2004/05 against interest income would not be worthwhile as it would merely waste the personal allowance. A s 380 ICTA 1988 claim in 2003/04 would also waste the personal allowance but it would allow a further claim to be made to set the loss against the chargeable gain in 2003/04. However, this would waste the CGT annual exemption and would save only £200 (£8,400 – £8,200) × 10% = £20 of CGT.

Alternatively, if a s 380 claim was not made for the 2003/04 loss in 2002/03, the 2004/05 loss could be carried back under s 381 ICTA 1988. £11,800 of the loss would be set off in 2002/03 and the balance in 2003/04 leaving taxable income in 2003/04 of £7,917. This is clearly less beneficial than the s 380 ICTA 1988 claim for the 2003/04 loss considered above.

A better alternative is to carry the 2004/05 loss forward for relief under s385 ICTA 1998 against Schedule D Case I profits of 2005/06:

	2005/06 £
Schedule D Case I	15,000
Less: s 385 relief	(13,333)
	1,667
Building society interest	3,800
	5,467

This leaves enough income in 2005/06 to absorb the personal allowance. Income tax is saved in 2005/06 on the whole of the loss set off.

(b) **The S380 ICTA 1988 claims for the 2003/04 loss must be made by the 31 January which is nearly two years after the end of the tax year of the loss: thus by 31 January 2006.**

There is no statutory time limit by which a claim to relieve a loss under S385 ICTA 1988 must be made. **However, a claim to establish the amount of the loss of 2004/05 to be carried forward must be made by the 31 January which is nearly 5 years after the end of the year of the loss: thus by 31 January 2010.** Once the loss is established, it will be carried forward and used where possible each year until used up.

Marking guide

			Marks
(a)	Schedule D I losses		
	2003/04		2
	2004/05		2
	Offset of loss		
		- S 380 ICTA 1988 2002/03	1
		- S 380 ICTA 1988 2003/04	1
	Order s 380 ICTA 1988 claims		1
	No s 380 ICTA 1988 2004/05		1
	Why no further s 380 or s 381 claims		2
	Carry forward under s 385		2
			12
(b)	S 380 time limit		1
	S 385 time limit		2
			3
			15

30   JACQUELINE

> **Tutor's hint.** It is important to realise that a terminal loss is calculated by splitting the last 12 months at 5 April. Overlap relief increases the loss arising after 5 April.

(a)   **Taxable profits**

	£
2000/01	
(1.5.00-5.4.01)	
£5,000 + 3/12 × £8,000	7,000
2001/02	
(Year to 31.12.01)	8,000
2002/03	
(Year to 31.12.02)	13,000
2003/04	
(Year to 31.12.03)	10,000
2004/05	
(Nine months to 30.9.04)	0

(b)   **Terminal loss relief**

The terminal loss is the loss from 1 October 2003 to 30 September 2004, as follows.

	£	£
6.4.04-30.9.04		
6/9 × (£14,500)		(9,667)
1.10.03-5.4.04		
1.10.03-31.12.03		
3/12 × £10,000	2,500	
1.1.04-5.4.04		
3/9 × (£14,500)	(4,833)	
		(2,333)
Overlap relief		(2,000)
Terminal loss		(14,000)

Relief is as follows.

	2000/01	*2001/02*	*2002/03*	*2003/04*	*2004/05*
	£	£	£	£	£
Original profits	7,000	8,000	13,000	10,000	0
Less terminal loss	0	0	(4,000)	(10,000)	0
Final profits	7,000	8,000	9,000	0	0
Total income	7,000	8,000	9,000	0	0

Marking guide

		Marks
(a)	2000/01	1
	2001/02	1
	2002/03	1
	2003/04	1
	2004/05	1
		5
(b)	Terminal loss calculation	
	- last 12 months	1
	- 6.4.04 – 30.9.04 calculation	4
	- 1.10.03 – 5.4.04 calculation	3
	Relief	
	- 03/04	1
	- 02/03	1
		10
		15

31 LOSSES AND CHANGE OF ACCOUNTING DATE

Tutor's hint. Remember to consider using the loss against gains as well as income.

(a) *2003/04*

It is clearly not beneficial to make a s 380 claim against total income as this would result in the loss of the personal allowance.

Income

	£
Sch DI (y/e 31.12.03)	2,500
Other income	2,500
STI	5,000
Less: PA	(4,745)
Taxable income	255

2004/05

A s 380 claim should be made, even though this results in the loss of the personal allowance. This is because the loss can be set against the capital gain.

Income

	£
Other income	2,900
Less: loss relief	(2,900)
STI/taxable income	Nil

Gains

	£
Gain	26,000
Less: c/y loss	(2,000)
	24,000

Less: loss relief lower of
(i) £(18,000 – 2,900) = £15,100;
(ii) £(24,000 – 4,700) = £19,300
ie

	£
	(15,100)
	8,900
Less: losses b/f	(700)
	8,200
Less: annual exemption	(8,200)
	Nil

Losses to c/f £(4,700 – 700)	£4,000

No trading loss to carry forward

(b)

2001/02
1.9.01 – 5.4.02
£16,000 + (3/12 × £48,000)   £28,000
2002/03
y/e 31.12.02   £48,000
2003/04
y/e 31.12.03   £36,000

Overlap profits are £12,000.
2004/05
1.1.04 – 31.3.05

42,000 + 15,000 (15 months)	57,000
Less: overlap profits (3 months)	(12,000)
Taxable profits	45,000

Marking guide

				Marks
(a)	2003/04	Taxable income	1	
		Reason not to use loss	2	
				3
	2004/05	Use s 380	1	
		Net gain	1	
		Loss relief max calculation	2	
		Capital losses b/f set off after trading loss	1	
		Annual exemption	½	
		Capital losses to c/f	½	
				6
(b)	2001/02		1	
	2002/03, 2003/04		2	
	2004/05		3	
				6
				15

32   PREPARATION QUESTION: PARTNERSHIPS

> **Tutor's hint.** Divide the profits of each accounting period between the partners before considering the amounts assessable in each tax year.

Each partner's share of the profits is

	Total £	Clare £	Justin £	Malcolm £
1.10.01–31.1.02	26,400	8,800	17,600	0
Y/e 31.1.03	60,000	20,000	40,000	0

Y/e 31.1.04

	Total	Clare	Justin	Malcolm
1.2.03–30.4.03 (3/12 × £117,000)	29,250		9,750	19,500	0
1.5.03–31.1.04 (9/12 × £117,000)	87,750		29,250	29,250	29,250
		117,000	39,000	48,750	29,250

Y/e 31.1.05

	Total	Clare	Justin	Malcolm
1.2.04–31.12.04 (11/12 × £108,108)	99,099		33,033	33,033	33,033
1.1.05–31.1.05 (1/12 × £108,108)	9,009		4,505	0	4,504
		108,108	37,538	33,033	37,537

The partners will be taxed on the above profits in the following tax years.

	Clare £	Justin £	Malcolm
2001/02 (1.10.01–5.4.02)			
1.10.01–31.1.02	8,800	17,600	
1.2.02–5.4.02 (2/12 × (£20,000/£40,000)	3,333	6,667	
	12,133	24,267	
2002/03 (Y/e 31.1.03)	£20,000	£40,000	
2003/04			
(Y/e 31.1.04)	£39,000	£48,750	
(1.5.03–5.4.04)			£
1.5.03-31.1.04			29,250
1.2.04-5.4.04 (2/12 × £37,537)			6,256
			35,506
2004/05			
(y/e 31.1.05)	£37,538		£37,537
(1.2.04–31.12.04)		33,033	
less: overlap relief		(6,667)	
		26,366	

Justin's overlap profits were relieved in the year he left the partnership. Clare and Malcolm have overlap profits that remain unrelieved of £3,333 and £6,256 respectively.

33 PARTNERSHIPS

> **Tutor's hint.** Overlap profits are relieved either on a change of accounting date or on a cessation. Each partner obtains relief for their own overlap profits and their own losses.

(a) Each partner is taxed like a sole trader who runs a business which starts when he joins the partnership; finishes when he leaves the partnership; has the same periods of account as the partnership; and makes profits or losses equal to the partner's share of the partnership profits or losses.

(b)

	Total £	Anne £	Betty £	Chloe £
1.1.04 – 31.12.04				
January to June	30,000	15,000	15,000	
July to December	30,000	15,000	-	15,000
Totals	60,000	30,000	15,000	15,000
1.1.05 – 31.12.05	72,000	36,000	-	36,000

Schedule DI assessments 2004/05

	Anne £	Betty £	Chloe £
Profits y/e 31.12.04	30,000		
Profits 1.1.04 – 30.6.04		15,000	
Profits 1.7.04 – 31.12.04			15,000
Profits 1.1.05 – 5.4.05			
3/12 × £36,000			9,000
	30,000	15,000	24,000
Less: overlap relief for Betty on cessation		(3,000)	
Profits assessable 2004/05	30,000	12,000	24,000

(c) (i) *Daniel*

Daniel can use his £20,000 loss:

- against total income of 2004/05 and/or of 2003/04 under s 380 ICTA 1988

- against future trading profits under s 385 ICTA 1988

(ii) *Edward*

Edward can use his £15,000 loss:

- against total income of 2004/05 and/or of 2003/04 under s 380 ICTA 1988

- if there is a terminal loss in the last 12 months of trading, against Schedule D Case II income of the tax year of cessation and the three preceding years, later years first, under s 388 ICTA 1988

(iii) *Frank*

Frank can use his loss of £5,000:

- against total income of 2004/05 and/or 2003/04 under s 380 ICTA 1988

- against total income of 2001/02, 2002/03 and 2003/04 under s 381 ICTA 1988

- against future trading profits under s 385 ICTA 1988

34 PREPARATION QUESTION: STAKEHOLDER PENSIONS

> **Tutor's hint.** The stakeholder pension scheme is extremely topical and highly likely to be examined.

(a) Maximum contributions

Tax year	Age at start of tax year	Basis year	%	Maximum contribution £
2004/05	42	2004/05	20	5,000
2005/06	43	2005/06	20	16,000
2006/07	44	2005/06	20	16,000
2007/08	45	2005/06	20	16,000
2008/09	46	2005/06	25	20,000
2009/10	47	2005/06	25	20,000
2010/11	48	2005/06	25	20,000
2011/12	49	2008/09	25	18,750

Note. The % depends on age at *start of the tax year of contribution* not on age at the start of the basis year.

(b) **Personal pension contributions are paid net of basic rate tax.** This means that for a basic rate taxpayer tax relief is given at source and there is no need to take any further action.

Higher rate taxpayers obtain additional relief through their personal tax computation. The basic rate band is extended by the gross amount of the pension contribution.

35 PREPARATION QUESTION: PERSONAL COMPUTATION

> **Tutor's hint.** Note that the % for personal pension purposes depends on Mr Thesaurus' age at the **start** of 2004/05.

(a) **Income tax computation**

	Non-savings £	Savings (excl. dividend) £	Dividend £	Total £
Schedule D Case I	56,000			
Dividend (£900 × 100/90)			1,000	
Bank interest £1,197 × 100/80		1,496		
	56,000	1,496	1,000	
Less charges: interest on loan	(6,000)			
STI	50,000	1,496	1,000	52,496
Less personal allowance	(4,745)			
	45,255	1,496	1,000	47,751

	£
Tax on non-savings income	
£2,020 × 10%	202
£29,380 × 22%	6,464
£13,855 (extended band) × 22%	3,048
Tax on savings (excl. dividend) income	
£1,145 (extended band) × 20%	229
£351 × 40%	140
Tax on dividend income	
£1,000 × 32.5%	325
Tax liability	10,408
Less tax suffered on bank interest £1,496 × 20%	(299)
tax credit on dividends £1,000 × 10%	(100)
Tax payable	10,009

(b) As 1999/00 was the basis year, the maximum gross pension premium relievable in 2004/05 is 20% × £80,000, ie £16,000.

The basic rate band is extended by the gross amount of the premium actually paid, £15,000 (£11,700 × $^{100}/_{78}$). ie £15,000 + £31,400 = £46,400

The interest paid on the loan to purchase a share in a partnership is eligible interest which qualifies for tax relief as a charge on income.

36 LAI CHAN

Tutor's hint. This question is a good example of the type of question that you might find on Section A of the exam.

1   For capital allowance purposes the WDA is restricted by the length of the basis period, but the FYA is not.

2   There is no capital allowance restriction in respect of the private use of an asset by an employee.

3   The basic rate band is extended by the gross amount of personal pension contributions made. Occupational pension contributions are, however, deducted in computing employment income.

(a) *Income tax liability 2004/05*

	£	*Non-savings income* £
Gross salary 9 × £3,250	29,250	
Less: pension contribution (6%)	(1,755)	
	27,495	
Car benefit (W1)	3,780	
Fuel benefit (W2)	2,700	
Taxable cheap loan (W3)	625	
Employment income		34,600
Trading profit	19,900	
Less: Capital allowances (W4)	(7,050)	
Schedule D Case II profit		12,850
STI		47,450
Less: personal allowance		(4,745)
Taxable income		42,705

Tax

	£
£2,020 × 10%	202
£29,380 × 22%	6,464
£390 × 100/78 × 3 (Extended Basic Rate Band) × 22%	330
£9,805 (42,705 – 31,400 – 1,500) × 40%	3,922
Tax liability	10,918

Workings

1   *Car benefit*

	£
25% × £26,400 × 9/12 (note)	4,950
Less: contribution £130 × 9	(1,170)
	3,780

Note. The % depends on the CO_2 emissions of the car.

CO_2 emissions = 195 g/km

Amount above baseline figure 195 – 145 = 50 g/km

Divide by 5 = 10 g/km

Taxable percentage = 15% + 10% = 25%

The benefit is time apportioned as the car is available for only nine months of the year.

2   *Fuel benefit*

£14,400 × 25% × 9/12   <u>£2,700</u>

No reduction for partial reimbursement of private fuel cost. The benefit is time apportioned as the car was available for only nine months of the year.

The taxable percentage used in calculating the fuel benefit is the same as the percentage used in calculating the car benefit.

3   *Taxable cheap loan*

Average method

$$5\% \times \frac{30,000 + 10,000}{2} \times 9/12 = \underline{£750}$$

Alternative method (strict method)

	£
£30,000 × 3/12 × 5% =	375
£10,000 × 6/12 × 5% =	<u>250</u>
	<u><u>625</u></u>

Elect for strict method

4   Capital allowances

	FYA £	General pool £	Private car (60%) £	Short life asset £	Allowances £
Additions not qualifying for FYA					
- private car			14,800		
- employee car		10,400			
WDA @ 25% × 3/12		<u>(650)</u>			650
		9,750			
WDA @ £3,000 (restricted) × 3/12			<u>(750)</u> × 60%		450
			14,050		
Additions qualifying for FYA					
- recording equipment	9,300				
- recording equipment				2,600	
Less: FYA @ 50%	<u>(4,650)</u>			(1,300)	5,950
TWDV c/f		<u>4,650</u>			
Allowances		<u>14,400</u>	<u>14,050</u>	<u>1,300</u>	
					<u>7,050</u>

(b) Up to 31 December 2004, PAYE will have been deducted from Lai Chan's salary. It is likely that her PAYE code was adjusted to take account of her benefits. Further tax payable (or tax repayable) will be dealt with under the self-assessment system.

As Lai Chan was employed before starting in business on her own account, she is unlikely to have made any payments on account for 2004/05. Therefore, the tax on her net Schedule D Case II profit will be collected in full on 31 January 2006 under the self assessment system.

37   CLAYTON DELANEY

> **Tutor's hint.** In this question, you should have dealt with the adjustment of profit for the final period, then the amount assessable on cessation and finally the personal tax computation.

(a)   **The adjustment of profit for the year ended 30 June 2004**

	£	£
Net profit per accounts		8,150
Additions		
Telephone £240 × 1/5	48	
Repairs: roof £650 × 2/3	433	
Repairs: bedroom	230	
Depreciation	1,350	
Buildings insurance £600 × 2/3	400	
Lighting and heating £420 × 2/3	280	
Car expenses £1,750 × ½	875	
Bad debts: loan written off	500	
Rates: council tax	650	
Proprietor's wages	11,850	
General expenses: gifts	900	
General expenses: donation to national charity	25	
Goods for own use £600 × 100/(100 − 20)	750	
	18,291	
		26,441
Deductions		
Interest received	300	
Profit on sale of shop fittings	20	
Capital allowances	3,440	
		(3,760)
Adjusted profit		22,681

Capital allowances

	Pool	Proprietor's car (50%)	Allowances
	£	£	£
Balances b/f	490	5,700	
Disposal		(4,500)	
Balancing allowance		1,200	600
Additions		9,000	
	490	9,000	
Proceeds	(400)	(3,500)	
Balancing (charge)/allowance	90	5,500	2,840
			3,440

Taxable profits

Year	Basis period	Profits
		£
2004/05	1.7.03 - 30.6.04	21,481

The final year's profits have been reduced by the overlap profits of £1,200.

(b) **Clayton: income tax computation**

	Non-savings	Savings (excl dividend) £	Total £
Salary £1,433.33 × 9	12,900		
Car benefit £10,000 × 19% × 9/12	1,425		
Fuel benefit £14,400 × 19% × 9/12	2,052		
Employment income	16,377		
Schedule D Case I	21,481		
BI £395 × 100/80		494	
Annuity £50 × 8		400	
Statutory total income	37,858	894	38,752
Less personal allowance	(4,745)		
Taxable income	33,113	894	34,007

	£
Income tax on non-savings income	
£2,020 × 10%	202
£29,380 × 22%	6,464
£1,713 × 40%	685
Income tax on savings (excl dividend) income	
£894 × 40%	358
Tax liability	7,709
Less tax suffered on annuity £400 × 20%	(80)
Less tax suffered on BI	(99)
Tax payable (subject to tax paid under PAYE)	7,530

Note. The CO2 emissions figure of the car is 150g/km rounded down to the nearest 5. This is 5g/km above the baseline figure of 145g/km so the taxable percentage is 16% + 3% (diesel) = 19%.

Marking Guide	Marks
(a)	
Adjustments to profit	
Telephone	1
Roof repairs	1
Bedroom repairs	1
Depreciation	1
Insurance/light and heat	1
Car expenses	1
Bad debts	1
Council tax	1
Wages	1
General expenses: gift	1
Donation to charity	1
Goods for own use	2
Profit on sale shop fittings/interest	1
Overlap relief	1
Taxable profits	1
Capital allowances computation	
Pool	1
Proprietor's car	2
	19
(b) Salary	1
Car benefit	2
Fuel benefit	1
Schedule D I	½
Bank interest	½
Annuity	1
Tax calculation	1
	7
	26

38 MARK KETT

> **Tutor's hint**. You need to take great care in identifying the rate of FYA available. It depends on the size of the business and the types and dates of the expenditure.

(a) **y/e 30.6.04**

	£
Adjusted profits	57,600
Less: capital allowances (W1)	(16,310)
Schedule D Case I	41,290

3 m/e 30.9.04

	£
Adjusted profits	17,400
Add: balancing charge (W1)	1,110
	18,510

Assessment for 2004/05

	£
y/e 30.6.04	41,290
3 m/e 30.9.04	18,510
	59,800
Less: overlap profits	(9,800)
	50,000

Note. It is important to be aware that you must always deduct capital allowances for each period of account before you begin allocating profits to tax years.

Working

1   *Capital allowances*

	FYA	Pool	Car × 60%	Allow-ances
	£	£	£	£
Y/e 30.06.04				
TWDV b/f		43,800	24,900	
WDA @ 25%		(10,950)		10,950
			(3,000) × 60%	1,800
		32,850	21,900	
Addition	8,900			
FYA @ 40%	(3,560)			3,560
		5,340		16,310
		38,190	21,900	
3 m/e 30.9.04				
Disposal		(43,200)	(15,400)	
		(5,010)	6,500	
Balancing charge/		5,010		(5,010)
Balancing allowance			(6,500) × 60%	3,900
				(1,110)

(b)

	Non-savings income	Dividend income	Total
	£	£	£
Schedule D Case I	50,000		
Employment income (W1)	37,000		
Dividends (× 100/90)		3,200	
	87,000	3,200	£90,200
Less: personal allowance	(4,745)		
Taxable income	82,255	3,200	£85,455

		£	£
Tax on non-savings income			
£2,020 × 10%			202
£29,380 × 22%			6,464
£50,855 × 40%			20,342
			27,008
Tax on dividend income			
£3,200 × 32.5%			1,040
			28,048
Less: PAYE (£1,890 x 6)		11,340	
Tax credit on dividends		320	
			(11,660)
Income tax payable			16,388
Less: payment on account			(24,400)
Repayment			(8,012)

(c) As Mark is **self employed records** relating to 2004/05 **must be retained until 5 years after the filing date,** ie until 31.1.10. **A failure to retain records for the required period may result in a penalty of up to £3,000.**

Working

Employment income

		£	£
Salary (£6,250 x 6)			37,500
Car	Allowance received	2,000	
	Authorised mileage allowance	(4,000)	
Excess			(2,000)
Loan (5% x £60,000 x 6/12)			1,500
Canteen (Note)			-
			37,000

Note 1. There is **no taxable benefit in respect of a staff canteen provided free meals are available to all staff on the same terms.**

Note 2. Mark Kett received a smaller mileage allowance (£2,000) than that given by the statutory mileage rates (£4,000). This means that the amount received by Mark Kett is tax free and there is a deduction for the excess of statutory allowance over the amount received.

39 PREPARATION QUESTION: A COTTAGE AND SHARES

> **Tutor's hint.** It is important to learn the matching rules for share transactions.

(a) **The cottage**

	£	£
Proceeds £(100,000 – 800)		99,200
Less: Indexed cost of property	49,625	
Indexed cost of extension	14,968	
		(64,593)
Indexed gain		34,607

As this is a non-business asset owned for seven years after 6.4.98 including the additional year, 75% of the gain is chargeable after taper relief, ie 75% × £34,607 = £25,955.

(b) **The disposal of shares in JVD Products plc**

Match disposals with acquisitions after 6 April 1998 on a LIFO basis:

(i) 12 August 2003 acquisition

	£
Disposal proceeds (500/4,000 × £40,000)	5,000
Less: cost	(2,000)
Chargeable gain (no taper relief)	3,000

(ii) 12 May 2001 acquisition

	£
Disposal proceeds (2,800/4,000 × £40,000)	28,000
Less: cost	(12,000)
Chargeable gain	16,000

The shares are a non-business asset so the gain after taper relief is 95% × £16,000 = £15,200. (The shares have been held for three complete years from 12.5.01.)

(iii) 1985 pool

	£
Proceeds (700/4,000 x £40,000)	7,000
Less: Indexed cost	(4,988)
Indexed gain	2,012

The shares are a non-business asset owned for seven years (including the bonus year) so the gain on the 1985 pool after taper relief is £1,509 (75% × £2,012).

Summary

	Gains
	£
12.8.03 acquisition	3,000
12.5.01 acquisition	15,200
1985 pool	1,509
Total gain on shares	19,709

(c)   **The tax liabilities**

	Non-savings £	Dividend £	Total £
Employment income	8,000		
Dividends £16,200 × 100/90	-	18,000	
STI	8,000	18,000	26,000
Less personal allowance	(4,745)		
Taxable income	3,255	18,000	21,255

	£
Income tax on non savings income	
£2,020 × 10%	202
£1,235 × 22%	272
Income tax on dividend income	
£18,000 × 10%	1,800
Tax liability	2,274

	£
Capital gains tax	
Gain on cottage	25,955
Gain on shares	19,709
	45,664
Less annual exemption	(8,200)
Taxable gains	37,464

	£
Capital gains tax liability	
£10,145 (£31,400 – £21,255) × 20%	2,029
£27,319 × 40%	10,928
£37,464	12,957

40   YVONNE, SALLY AND JOANNE

> **Tutor's hint.** Always set losses against gains attracting the lowest rate of taper relief. The set off of losses is made before the deduction of taper relief.

(a)   The sale of Yvonne's shares is initially matched with the shares bought in the next 30 days.

	£
Proceeds (1,000/5,000 × £23,000)	4,600
Less: cost (28.3.05)	(4,400)
Chargeable gain	200

No taper relief.

Next the shares are matched with the post 6.4.98 acquisition.

	£
Proceeds (2,000/5,000 × £23,000)	9,200
Less: cost (19.9.02)	(5,000)
Gain	4,200

No taper relief due.

Finally the shares are matched with the FA1985 pool.

	£
Disposal proceeds (2,000/5,000)	9,200
Less: cost (2,000/3,000 × £6,000)	(4,000)
	5,200
Less: indexation (2,000/3,000 (6,510 – 6,000))	(340)
Gain before taper relief	4,860
Gain after taper relief (75%)	3,645

These shares have been held for 7 years (including the bonus year) hence 7.5% taper relief.

Yvonne's total gain before the annual exemption is £8,045.

(b)

	£
Capital gain on non-business asset (no taper relief)	10,000
Less: capital loss in year	(6,000)
capital loss b/f	(4,000)
	–

	£
Capital gain on business asset	41,000
Less: capital loss b/f (£12,000 – £4,000)	(8,000)
Gain before taper relief	33,000
Gain after taper relief (25%) (owned 2+ years)	8,250

The losses are initially allocated to the gain on which no taper relief is due as this maximises the taper relief on the other gain.

The gain remaining chargeable after taper relief and the annual exemption is £50 (£8,250 – £8,200).

(c)

Business use		
1.8.02 – 1.8.03	=	12 months
Non business use		
1.8.03 – 1.2.05	=	18 months
		30 months

Number of complete years of ownership 1.8.02 – 31.7.04 = 2 years

	£
Business element	
£50,000 × 12/30 × 25%	5,000
Non business element	
£50,000 × 18/30 × 100%	30,000
Gain after taper relief	35,000

Marking Guide	Marks	
(a) Match with shares bought in next 30 days	1	
Gain	1	
Match with post April 1998 acquisition	1	
Gain	1	
Match with FA 1985 pool shares	1	
Gain	2	
Total gain	1	
		8
(b) Set losses against gain on non-business asset	1	
Set balance of brought forward loss against gain on business asset	1	
Taper relief after set off losses	1	
Gain chargeable	1	
		4
(c) Business/non business use	1	
Ownership period of taper relief	1	
Taper relief	1	
		3
		15

41   JACK CHAN

> **Tutor's hint**. The brought forward loss must be set against the gain that suffers the lowest rate of taper relief.

Goodwill

	£
Market value	60,000
Less: cost	-
	60,000
Less: gift relief	(10,000)
Gain immediately chargeable	50,000

The amount paid for the goodwill exceeds allowable cost by £50,000, so £50,000 is immediately chargeable. The goodwill is a business asset that has been owned for more than 2 years so 25% of the gain remains after taper relief.

Office

	£
Market value	130,000
Less: cost	(110,000)
	20,000
Less: gift relief	(20,000)
Gain immediately chargeable	-

As the amount paid for the office was less than the allowable cost, gift relief is available to defer the whole gain arising.

Warehouse

	£
Market value	140,000
Less: cost	(95,000)
Gain chargeable	45,000

This is a non-business asset held for two years only, so no taper relief is due. In addition, gift relief is not available to defer a gain on a non business asset.

Motor car

The motor car is an exempt asset, so no gain or loss arises.

Total gains

	£	£
Goodwill (£50,000 × 25%)		12,500
Warehouse	45,000	
Less: loss	(6,400)	
		38,600
		51,100
Less: annual exemption		(8,200)
Taxable gains		42,900

CGT

	£
£7,800 (£31,400 - £23,600) × 20%	1,560
£35,100 × 40%	14,040
£42,900	
CGT due on 31.1.06	15,600

CGT of £15, 600 must be paid by 31.1.06.

Marking guide	Marks
Goodwill	
Gift relief	2
Gain chargeable after taper	1
Office	
Gift relief	2
Warehouse	
Gain	1
No gift relief	1
No taper relief	1
Car – exempt	1
Set off loss	2
Annual exemption	1
CGT	2
Due date	1
	15

42   MR EDWARDS

> **Tutor's hint.** You were required to prepare notes for a meeting, so you could put your answer in note format.

(a) **Registration for VAT**

- A person making taxable supplies becomes liable to register for VAT if, in any period of up to 12 consecutive calendar months, the value of his taxable supplies (excluding VAT) exceeds £58,000. The person is required to notify Customs within 30 days of the end of the 12 month period. Customs will then register the person with effect from the end of the month following the 12 month period, or from an earlier date if they and the trader agree.

- Turnover exceeded the registration limit of £58,000 by 31 October 2004 and registration was therefore necessary by 1 December 2004.

- Immediate registration is now necessary.

- There is a VAT liability on any sales made since 1 December 2004.

- VAT should be charged immediately and customers advised that VAT invoices will be issued when the VAT registration number is known.

- VAT on sales from 1 December to today (10 December) will have to be accounted for out of Mr Edward's profit margin.

(b) **Annual accounting**

- The annual accounting scheme is available to traders whose taxable turnover (exclusive of VAT) for the twelve months starting on their application to join the scheme is not expected to exceed £660,000.

- Traders cannot usually apply to join the scheme until they have been registered for at least twelve months. However, if Mr Edwards has a taxable turnover of up to £150,000 he can join the scheme as soon as he is registered.

- At the end of the year the trader compiles an annual VAT return which must be submitted to Customs along with any balancing payment of VAT (see below) due by two months after the end of the year.

- Throughout the year payments on account of VAT must be made by direct debit. The trader must pay 90% of the previous year's net VAT liability during the year by means of nine monthly payments commencing at the end of the fourth month of the year.

Marking guide

		Marks
(a)		
	Turnover limit exceeded by 31 October	3
	Register immediately (effective date 1 December)	2
	Liability to VAT from 1 December	1
	VAT to be charged immediately and invoices later	2
	Sales 1.12 – 10.12 – profit margin	1
(b)	Annual accounting turnover limit	1
	12 month rule/£150,000 limit	2
	One return and due date	2
	Monthly payments on account	1
		15

43   PREPARATION QUESTION: BENEFITS

Tutor's hint. It was important to note that the car was acquired part way through the year and to time apportion the benefit accordingly.

(a)   **The use of a private house which cost £120,000**

Two calculations are required.

(i)   The living accommodation benefit

	£
Annual value	2,000
Less contribution by director	(2,000)
	0

(ii)   The additional charge for expensive accommodation

£(120,000 – 75,000) × 5%	£2,250

The total benefit is £2,250.

(b)   **The purchase of a company asset at an undervalue**

The **benefit is the greater** of:

(i)   The **asset's current market value**, and

(ii)   The **asset's market value when first provided, less the total benefits taxed during the period of use**.

The acquisition price paid by the director is deducted from whichever of (i) and (ii) is used.

	£	£
Market value when first provided		3,500
Less: taxed in 2000/01 (20% of market value)	700	
taxed in 2001/02 (20% of market value)	700	
taxed in 2002/03 (20%)	700	
taxed in 2003/04 (20%)	700	
		(2,800)
		700

The figure of £700 is taken (as greater than the current market value of £600).

Benefit taxed in 2004/05

	£
Initial market value minus benefits already taxed	700
Less amount paid by director	(600)
Benefit	100

(c) **A low-interest loan to a director to purchase a season ticket**

This non qualifying loan is exempt as the total of all non qualifying loans to this director does not exceed £5,000.

(d) **The provision of medical insurance**

The residual charge applies to the taxable value of this benefit as the director is not an excluded employee. The value of the tax benefit is the cost of the benefit to the employer. The benefit is thus £800.

(e) **Mercedes car**

The car was available for only seven months of the year so the benefit must be on a time basis. The fuel benefit must be dealt with similarly.

The taxable percentage is 15% for cars with a baseline CO_2 emissions figure of 145g/km. This % is increased by 1% for every additional 5g/km of CO_2 emissions. In this case the % is 35%.

£24,000 × 35% × 7/12	£4,900
The fuel benefit is £14,400 × 35% × 7/12	£2,940

(f) **Computer**

	£
£3,900 × 20%	780
Less: de minimis	(500)
	280

44 RITA

> **Tutor's hint.** Always take care to apportion car and fuel benefits correctly. The CO_2 emissions figure for the car is rounded down to the nearest five below. 145g/km is the baseline figure at which the taxable percentage is 15%. The percentage is increased by 1% for each 5g/km by which the CO_2 emissions figure exceeds 145g/km.

	£
Salary	48,000
Accommodation (W1)	21,200
Relocation (£12,000 – £8,000)	4,000
Loan (£10,000 × 5%)	500
Car (£18,500 × 15% × 8/12)	1,850
Fuel benefit (£14,400 × 15% × 8/12)	1,440
Employment income	76,990

Workings

1   *Accommodation*

	£
Annual value (higher than rent paid)	4,000
Electricity	700
Gas	1,200
Water	500
Council tax	1,300
Repairs	3,500
Furniture (20% × £30,000 × 6/12)	3,000
Purchase (W2)	7,000
	21,200

2   *Purchase of furniture*

Benefit is the higher of:

		£
(i)	Cost	30,000
	Less: taxed	(3,000)
		27,000
	Less: amount paid	(20,000)
		7,000
(ii)	Market value	25,000
	Less: amount paid	(20,000)
		5,000

ie £7,000

Marking Guide

	Marks
Salary	1
Higher of annual value & rent	1
Ancillary services	2
Relocation	1
Use of furniture	1
Purchase of furniture (W2)	2
Loan	2
Car	3
Fuel	2
	15

---

45   JOSEPHINE

> **Tutor's hint.** The calculation of car and fuel benefits are very important as they are often examined.

(a)   Class 1 primary contributions payable by Josephine

11% × £(402 – 91) × 52   £1,778.92

Class 1 secondary contributions - payable by employer

12.8% × £(402 – 91) × 52   £2,070.02

Class 1A contributions - payable by employer

£6,670 (W1) × 12.8%   £853.76

Note. **Childcare is exempt from Class 1 NICs provided it arises as a result of a contract made by the employer, not just reimbursed to the employee.** From 6 April 2005 employers may make a payment of up to £50 per week free of NIC and income tax.

Working

1   *Benefits*

	£
Car 1 £12,000 × 8/12 × 25%	2,000
Car 2 £21,000 × 4/12 × 15%	1,050
Fuel - Car 1 £14,400 × 25% × 8/12	2,400
Fuel - Car 2 £14,400 × 15% × 4/12	720
Medical insurance	500
	6,670

Note. For Car 1, the CO_2 emissions figure is rounded down to 180/km. The baseline percentage is increased by 1% for each multiple of 5g/km above 145g/km. In this case 15% + 7% = 22%.

The percentage is then increased by 3% because the car is a diesel-engined car.

Marking guide

	Marks
Class 1A – on benefits	1
Class 1 - primary	2
Class 1 - secondary	2
Childcare	2
	7
Working	
Car 1 - Benefit	
25%	2
Time apportion	1
	3
Car 2 - Benefit	
15%	1
Time apportion	1
	2
Fuel benefit - Car 1	1
Fuel benefit - Car 2	1
Medical insurance	1
	3
	15

46   APPLEBY PIES

(i)   **Cessation of trade for income tax**

When an unincorporated trade is transferred to a company, **the trade is treated as ceasing for income tax purposes**.

The **basis period for the final tax year runs from the end of the basis period for the previous year to the date of cessation**.

The date of cessation should be chosen carefully to avoid large taxable profits in one year from a basis period of more than 12 months.

If there are **overlap profits, these can be relieved on cessation**.

(ii)   **Capital allowances**

On a transfer of assets to the company, **a balancing charge will usually arise** as plant and machinery are treated as sold at market value.

However, where the company is controlled by the transferor, the two are connected and **an election can be made not to treat the transfer as a permanent discontinuance. Fixed assets are then transferred at tax written down value.**

(iii)   **Trading losses**

Unrelieved trading losses cannot be carried forward against company profits.

However, they **can be set against income derived from the company** such as remuneration, dividends and interest received from the company.

(iv)   **Capital gains tax**

When the transfer of the business takes place there will be a **disposal of chargeable assets** (eg land, goodwill) **at market value** by the trader.

Business asset taper relief will apply to reduce the gains.

If the whole business (or the whole business other than cash) is transferred in exchange for shares, any chargeable gains (before taper relief) are rolled over against the base cost of the shares. This is known as **incorporation relief**.

Alternatively, **gift relief can be used to transfer chargeable assets to the company** and defer gains by deducting them against the base cost of the assets in the company.

(v)   **Value added tax**

The transfer of assets would be treated as a supply for VAT.

However, the transfer will not be treated as a supply under the **Transfer of Going Concern Relief** if:

(i)   the assets are to be used by the company in the same kind of business and the business is transferred as a **going concern** or if only part is transferred, it is capable of separate operation:

(ii)   **if the transferor is a taxable person, the company is a taxable person when the transfer takes place or immediately becomes one as a result of the transfer.**

Deregister sole trader business and register company for VAT.

Marking guide

		Marks
(i)	Ceasing to trade	1
	Basis periods	1
	Overlap profits	1
		3
(ii)	Market value disposal	1
	Balancing adjustments	1
	Election	1
		3
(iii)	No carry forward	1
	Offset vs Co income	2
		3
(iv)	Disposal at market value	1
	Incorporation relief	1
	Gift relief	1
		3
(v)	Supply of assets	1
	TOGC relief	1
	Admin – deregister business and register Co	1
		3
		15

47   JANE JONES

> **Tutor's hint**. This question was a very popular optional question when it was set. The examiner said the question was very well done.

(a) (i)   **Employment with Aurora plc**

	£
Salary	30,000
Car (£18,400 × 22% (W1))	4,048
Use of car (£50 × 12)	(600)
Petrol £14,400 x 22%	3,168
STI	36,616
Less: personal allowance	(4,745)
Taxable income	31,871

Tax	£
£2,020 × 10%	202
£29,380 × 22%	6,464
£471 × 40%	188
Income tax liability	6,854

Workings

Car and fuel benefit

180 g/km (rounded down) – 145 g/km = 35 g/km

÷ 5 = 7 g/km

Taxable percentage

15% + 7% = 22%

(ii) **Employment with Zodiac plc**

	£	£
Salary		32,000
Mileage allowance (10,000 × 20p)	2,000	
Less: authorised mileage rates (10,000 × 40p)	(4,000)	
Expense claim for excess		(2,000)
STI		30,000
Less: personal allowance		(4,745)
Taxable income		25,255

Tax	£
£2,020 × 10%	202
£23,235 × 22%	5,112
	5,314

(b) If Jane accepts the employment offer from Aurora plc, she will have net income of £23,146 (£30,000 – £6,854). She will incur expenses of £600 in respect of the car.

If the offer from Zodiac plc is accepted net income is £28,686 (£32,000 + £2,000 – £5,314). However, the motor running costs will be £7,100.

Overall the offer from Aurora plc is better. Net income is £5,540 lower but this is more than offset by the fact that motor expenses are £6,500 lower.

Marking guide

		Marks	
(a)	**Offer of employment from Aurora plc**		
	Salary	½	
	Car benefit	2	
	Fuel benefit	1	
	Personal allowance	½	
	Income tax	1	
			5
(b)	**Offer of employment from Zodiac plc**		
	Salary	½	
	Mileage allowance	1	
	Authorised mileage rates	2	
	Personal allowance	½	
	Income tax	1	
			5
(c)	Aurora plc: net income/care costs	2	
	Zodiac plc: net income/car costs	2	
	Conclusion	1	
			5
			15

---

48 CAROL COURIER

Tutor's hint. This was a very straightforward question which really should have given you no trouble.

(a)

	Non-savings income £
Salary	26,000
Pension (5%)	(1,300)
	24,700
Less: personal allowance	(4,745)
Taxable income	19,955

Tax

	£
£2,020 × 10%	202
£17,935 × 22%	3,946
19,955	4,148

Class 1 NICs

	£
(£26,000 – 4,745) × 11% =	£2,338

(b)

	£
Schedule D Case I (£38,000 + £8,500 – £4,400 - £2,800)	39,300
Less: personal allowance	(4,745)
Taxable income	34,555

Tax

	£
£2,020 × 10%	202
£29,380 × 22%	6,464
£2,000 [extended band] × 22%	440
£1,155 x 40%	462
	7,568

Class 2 NICs (52 x £2.05)=	£107

	£
Class 4 (£31,720 – 4,745) × 8% =	2,158
£(39,300 – 31,720) x 1%	76
	2,234

(c) **Employment**

	£
Salary	26,000
Pension	(1,300)
Tax	(4,148)
NICs	(2,338)
Net income	18,214

Self employment

	£
Net income	39,300
Less: Pension paid (£2,000 x 78%)	(1,560)
Tax	(7,568)
Class 2 NICs	(107)
Class 4 NICs	(2,234)
Net income	27,831

∴ Carol's income will increase by £9,617 if she works on a self employed basis.

Marking guide

		Marks
(a)	Salary	½
	Pension	1
	Personal allowance	½
	Tax	1
	Class 1 NIC	2
		5
(b)	Net income	1
	Personal allowance	½
	Tax	1½
	Class 4 NIC	2
	Class 2 NIC	1
		6
(c)	Net income if employed	1
	Net income if self employed	2
	Conclusion	1
		4
		15

49   MR ROYLE

Tutor's hint. The mention of losses in the question should lead you to consider whether it is possible to utilise them in future.

1 High Street
Anywhere

Mr J Royle
Blues House
Anywhere

[Date]

Dear Mr Royle

Purchase of business

Thank you for your enquiry about your proposed purchase. I will outline the advantages of either buying the assets of the business or shares in the company.

Purchase of assets

(a) You will be able to choose which assets you wish to acquire, rather than the whole of the assets of the company.

(b) You will be entitled to claim **capital allowances on plant and machinery, including possible first year allowances of 50% depending on the type of asset acquired. Industrial buildings allowance may also be available on the factory**.

(c) It may be possible to **maximise the use of capital allowances by allocating consideration to assets which attract more capital allowances,** eg plant and machinery.

(d) The liabilities of the company will not be passed to you.

(e) One disadvantage is that you **will not be able to utilise the existing losses of the company**.

(f) **VAT may be chargeable on the assets** acquired by you. If you cannot fully recover all the VAT paid on acquiring the assets, this may be unattractive.

There is a relief which provides that VAT is not chargeable on the transfer of a business as a going concern, but this may not be available if you only purchase some of the assets.

Purchase of shares

(a) The business of the company will continue uninterrupted.

(b) You will be taking over the liabilities of the company as well as the assets.

(c) **Capital allowances and industrial buildings allowance will be unaffected** by the purchase. However, this means that there will be no first year allowances available.

(d) It may be possible **for the losses incurred by the company to be carried forward** and used against profits in future years.

However, **where there is a change in ownership of a company and a major change in the nature of the conduct of the company's trade occurs within three years, trading losses cannot be carried forward**. This also applies where there is a change in ownership after the scale of activities has become small or negligible before it revives.

I suggest we meet to discuss your proposed purchase further.

Yours sincerely,

Certified Accountant

Marking guide

		Marks
Layout		1
(a)	Choose which assets	1
	Capital allowances and IBAs	2
	Consideration	1
	No liabilities	1
	No use of losses	1
	VAT charge	1
	TOGC relief	1
		8
(b)	Business carries on	1
	Liabilities transferred	1
	Capital allowances and IBAs	1
	Losses used	1
	Restriction on losses	2
		6
		15

50   ABDUL PATEL

> **Tutor's hint.** It was important not to ignore the fact that only £25,000 of the basic rate band was available. This approach was used by the examiner to simplify the repetitive income tax calculations.

(a)   Class 2 NICs
£2.05 × 52 = £106.60
Class 4 NICs

	£
8% × (£31,720 – £4,745)	2,158
1% × (£80,000 – £31,720)	483
	2,641

Income tax	£
£25,000 × 22%	5,500
£55,000 × 40%	22,000
Income tax liability	27,500

(b)   (i)   CT Liability

	£
Profits	80,000
Remuneration	(45,000)
Class 1 NICs	
(£45,000 – £4,745) × 12.8%	(5,153)
	29,847

	£
CT @ 19%	5,671
Less 19/400 (50,000 – 29,847)	(957)
	4,714

Abdul's income tax liability:

	£
£25,000 × 22%	5,500
£20,000 × 40%	8,000
	13,500

Abdul's Class 1 NICs:

	£
(£31,720 – £4,745) × 11%	2,967
(£45,000 – £31,720) × 1%	133
	3,100

(ii)   Dividends £45,000
CT liability
£80,000 × 19% = £15,200
Abdul's income tax liability

Dividends £45,000 × $\dfrac{100}{90}$ = £50,000

	£
£25,000 × 10%	2,500
£25,000 32.5%	8,125
	10,625
Less: tax credit on dividends	(5,000)
	5,625

Marking guide

			Marks
(a)	Income tax liability		1
	Class 2 NIC		1
	Class 4 NIC		2
			4
(b)	(i) Director's remuneration		
	Class 1 NIC - Secondary		2
	Corporation tax - PCTCT		1
	- Liability		1
	Income tax liability		1
	Class 1 NIC - Primary		2
			7
	(ii) Dividends		
	Corporation tax liability		1
	Income tax - Gross dividends		1
	- Liability		2
			4
			15

51   INCORPORATION

> **Tutor's hint.** Make sure you cover all parts of this question instead of writing too much on any one part.

(a)   **Cessation of trade for income tax**

When an unincorporated trade is transferred to a company, **the trade is treated as ceasing for income tax purposes.**

The **basis period for the final tax year runs from the end of the basis period for the previous year to the date of cessation.**

The date of cessation should be chosen carefully to avoid large taxable profits in one year from a basis period of more than 12 months.

If there are **overlap profits, these can be relieved on cessation.**

(b)   **Capital allowances**

On a transfer of assets to the company, **a balancing charge will usually arise** as plant and machinery are treated as sold at market value.

However, where the company is controlled by the transferor, the two are connected and **an election can be made not to treat the transfer as a permanent discontinuance. Fixed assets are then transferred at tax written down value.**

(c)   **Trading losses**

Unrelieved trading losses cannot be carried forward against company profits.

However, they **can be set against income derived from the company** such as remuneration, dividends and interest received from the company.

(d)   **Capital gains tax**

When the transfer of the business takes place there will be a **disposal of chargeable assets** (eg land, goodwill) **at market value** by the trader.

Business asset taper relief will apply to reduce the gains.

BPP
PROFESSIONAL EDUCATION

If the whole business (or the whole business other than cash) is transferred in exchange for shares, any chargeable gains (before taper relief) are rolled over against the base cost of the shares. This is known as **incorporation relief**.

Alternatively, **gift relief can be used to transfer chargeable assets to the company** and defer gains by deducting them against the base cost of the assets in the company.

(e) **Value added tax**

The transfer of assets would be treated as a supply for VAT.

However, the transfer will not be treated as a supply under the **Transfer of Going Concern Relief** if:

(i)   the assets are to be used by the company in the same kind of business and the business is transferred as a **going concern** or if only part is transferred, it is capable of separate operation:

(ii) **if the transferor is a taxable person, the company is a taxable person when the transfer takes place or immediately becomes one as a result of the transfer.**

Marking guide

			Marks
(a)	Cessation of business	1	
	Basis period	1	
	Choice of date	1	
	Overlap profits	1	
			4
(b)	Balancing charge	1	
	Election to transfer at TWDV	1	
			2
(c)	No c/f losses	1	
	Set against income from company	1	
			2
(d)	Gain on chargeable assets	1	
	Taper relief	1	
	Incorporation relief	1	
	Gift relief	1	
			4
(e)	Supply of goods	1	
	TOGC	2	
			3
			15

Business Taxation
Mock Exam 1

Question Paper:	
Time allowed	**3 hours**
This paper is divided into two sections	
Section A	**BOTH questions MUST be answered**
Section B	**THREE questions ONLY to be answered**

paper 2.3

DO NOT OPEN THIS PAPER UNTIL YOU ARE READY TO START
UNDER EXAMINATION CONDITIONS

SECTION A – BOTH questions are compulsory and MUST be attempted

52   UNUSUAL URNS LTD

(a) Unusual Urns Limited (UUL) is a United Kingdom resident company which manufactures pottery. It has no associated companies.

The company's results for the year ended 31 January 2005 were as follows.

	£
Trading profits (as adjusted for taxation but before capital allowances)	900,000
Income	
Bank interest (note 2)	5,000
Loan interest (note 3)	40,000
Expenditure	
Gift aid donation (note 4)	20,000

Notes

1   UUL is a medium-sized company with a turnover in the year ended 31 January 2005 of £8,000,000. The average number of employees during the accounting period was 120.

2   *Bank interest*

		£
31.7.04	Received	2,000
31.1.05	Received	3,000
		5,000

The interest was non-trading income. There were no accrued amounts at the beginning or end of the year.

3   *Loan interest*

		£
31.7.04	Received	20,000
31.1.05	Received	20,000
		40,000

(a) The interest was received gross from another UK company
(b) The interest was non-trading income
(c) The loan was made on 1 April 2004
(d) There were no accrued amounts at the end of the year.

4   *Gift aid donation*

The gift aid donation was paid on 1 July 2004.

5   *Plant and machinery*

On 1 February 2004 the tax written down values of plant and machinery were as follows.

	£
Pool	223,000
'Short-life' asset	2,500
Expensive car (1)	16,000

During the year ended 31 January 2005 the following capital transactions took place.

Purchases

		£
1.4.04	Machinery	280,000
1.8.04	Expensive car (2)	35,000
1.9.04	Machinery	45,000
1.10.04	Cars (not 'expensive')	60,000
1.12.04	Lorry	55,000

Sales

		£
1.5.04	Machinery	40,000
1.8.04	Expensive car (1)	18,000
1.10.04	Cars (not 'expensive')	20,000
1.11.04	Short-life asset (purchased 31.12.01)	500

Notes

(1) The two purchases of machinery and the lorry are not to be treated as either 'short-life' assets or 'long-life' assets.

(2) No asset was sold for an amount greater than cost.

(3) None of the machinery acquired was computer or information technology equipment.

(4) None of the cars are low emission cars.

6   *Industrial buildings*

During 2000 UUL had erected a factory which was brought into use in December 2000. The costs incurred were as follows.

	£
Land	60,000
Legal expenses on acquisition of land	3,000
Levelling land	2,000
Factory	100,000
Architect's fees on construction of factory	6,000

Included in the costs of the factory were administrative offices (£10,000) and a design office (£5,000).

In August/September 2004 the administration offices were extended at a cost of £30,000.

Required

Calculate the corporation tax payable for the year ended 31 January 2005 and state the due date for the payment of the tax.   (22 marks)

(b) The results of Unusual Urns Limited for the previous two accounting periods were as follows.

	Year ended 31.7.03 £	6 months to 31.1.04 £
Schedule D		
Case I profit/(loss)	210,000	(150,000)
Charges on income:		
Gift aid donations	7,500	10,000

Required

(i)   State the alternative methods by which UUL can obtain relief for the loss of £150,000 sustained in the period ended 31 January 2004; and

(ii)   State, with your reasons, which of the alternative loss utilisation methods you have described in (b)(i) above you would choose to obtain the maximum tax advantage when claiming loss relief in respect of the £150,000 loss. You should also state what effect your proposed treatment of the losses will have on the charges on income paid. (8 marks)

(30 marks)

Notes

1   Calculations are not required in part (b).

2   None of the information provided in part (b) of the question is to be taken into account when answering part (a) of the question.

53   **WILLIAM WISE**

On 1 June 2004 William Wise, aged 38, commenced in self-employment running a retail clothing shop. William's profit and loss account for the year ended 31 May 2005 is as follows:

	£	£
Gross profit		139,880
Expenses		
Depreciation	4,760	
Light and heat (note 1)	1,525	
Motor expenses (note 2)	4,720	
Professional fees (note 3)	2,300	
Rent and rates (note 1)	3,900	
Repairs and renewals (note 4)	5,660	
Sundry expenses (note 5)	2,990	
Wages and salaries (note 6)	83,825	
		(109,680)
Net profit		30,200

Note 1 – Private accommodation

William and his wife live in a flat that is situated above the clothing shop. Of the expenditure included in the profit and loss account for light, heat, rent and rates, 40% relates to the flat.

Note 2 – Motor expenses

During the year ended 31 May 2005 William drove a total of 12,000 miles, of which 9,000 were for private journeys.

Note 3 – Professional fees

Professional fees are as follows:

	£
Accountancy	700
Legal fees in connection with the purchase of the clothing shop	1,200
Debt collection	400
	2,300

Included in the figure for accountancy is £250 in respect of personal tax work for 2003/04.

Note 4 – Repairs and renewals

The figure of £5,660 for repairs and renewals includes £2,200 for decorating the clothing shop during May 2004, and £1,050 for decorating the private flat during June 2004. The building was in a usable state when it was purchased.

Note 5 – Sundry expenses

The figure of £2,990 for sundry expenses includes £640 for gifts to customers of food hampers costing £40 each, £320 for gifts to customers of pens carrying an advertisement for the clothing shop costing £16 each, £100 for a donation to a national charity, and £40 for a donation to a local charity's fete. The fete's programme carried a free advertisement for the clothing shop.

Note 6 – Wages and salaries

The figure of £83,825 for wages and salaries includes the annual salary of £15,500 paid to William's wife. She works in the clothing shop as a sales assistant. The other sales assistants doing the same job are paid an annual salary of £11,000.

Note 7 – Goods for own use

During the year ended 31 May 2005 William took clothes out of the shop for his personal use without paying for them. The cost of these clothes was £460, and they had a selling price of £650.

Note 8 – Plant and machinery

William purchased the following assets:

		£
10 May 2004	Fixtures and fittings	19,520
1 June 2004	Motor car	14,000
3 July 2004	Computer	5,100

The fixtures and fittings all qualify as plant and machinery for capital allowances purposes. The motor car is used by William.

William's business is a small enterprise for capital allowance purposes

Other information

William was employed by Haberdasher plc as a manager from 6 April 1997 until 5 April 2004. He was paid a salary of £48,000 p.a., and was not a member of Haberdasher plc's occupational pension scheme.

During 2004/05 William received dividends of £6,750 (net).

Required

(a) Calculate William's tax adjusted Schedule DI profit for the year ended 31 May 2005. (14 marks)

(b) Calculate William's income tax and Class 4 NIC liability for 2004/05. (5 marks)

(c) Advise William of

   (i)   the maximum amount that he can contribute to a personal pension scheme for 2004/05;

   (ii) the date by which the contribution must be paid; and

   (iii) the method by which tax relief will be given for the contribution. You should assume that today's date is 15 June 2005. (6 marks)

(25 marks)

SECTION B - THREE questions ONLY to be attempted

54   REGISTRATION, ERRORS AND DEREGISTRATION

(a) Confused Ltd will commence trading in the near future. The company operates a small aeroplane, and is considering three alternative types of business. These are (1) training, in which case all sales will be standard rated for VAT, (2) transport, in which case all sales will be zero-rated for VAT, and (3) an air ambulance service, in which case all sales will be exempt from VAT.

For each alternative Confused Ltd's sales will be £75,000 per month (exclusive of VAT), and standard rated expenses will be £10,000 per month (inclusive of VAT).

Required

For each of the three alternative types of business (i) state whether Confused Ltd will be required or permitted to register for VAT when trading commences, and (ii) calculate the monthly amount of output VAT due and input VAT recoverable.   (6 marks)

(b) Puzzled Ltd has discovered that a number of errors have been made when preparing its VAT returns for the previous four quarters. As a result of the errors the company will have to make an additional payment of VAT to Customs.

Required

Explain how Puzzled Ltd can voluntarily disclose the errors that have been discovered, and whether default interest will be due, if the net errors in total are (i) less than £2,000, or (ii) more than £2,000.   (3 marks)

(c) Perplexed Ltd has been registered for VAT since 1997, but intends to cease trading on 31 December 2005. On the cessation of trading Perplexed Ltd can either sell its fixed assets on a piecemeal basis to individual purchasers, or it can sell its entire business as a going concern to a single purchaser.

Required

Advise Perplexed Ltd as to what will happen to its VAT registration, and whether output VAT will be due, if the company ceases trading on 31 December 2005 and then (i) sells its fixed assets on a piecemeal basis, or (ii) sells its entire business as a going concern.   (6 marks)

(15 marks)

55   ABC LTD

ABC Ltd, a UK resident company which manufactures concrete slabs, owns 8,000 shares in DEF Ltd, an investment company. This holding represents 80% of the share capital of DEF Ltd.

ABC Ltd needs to raise approximately £510,000 in order to repay a loan which is due for repayment in June 2005.

The directors of the company advised you in October 2004 that they were considering the sale of two assets, each of which could be sold for £700,000. They sought your advice on which of the two assets would generate sufficient funds, after taking into account any corporation tax payable on the resultant gain, to repay the outstanding loan. It was the directors' intention to sell the appropriate asset in

December 2004, during ABC Ltd's accounting period of twelve months to 31 March 2005.

Details of the two assets, only ONE of which was to be sold, are as follows;

(a) A plot of land which had cost £130,000 in June 1997 and which is used for the storage of finished products.

This purchase had been funded by the sale in May 1996, for £140,000, of another plot of land, used for parking the company's vehicles. This land had cost £80,000 in May 1989.

On the occasion of this first sale, the maximum possible rollover relief was claimed.

(b) The 80% holding of shares in DEF Ltd.

These shares had cost £40,000 in May 1990.

Prior to the current proposed disposal, ABC Ltd had not made any other disposals since May 1996.

You establish that ABC Ltd's other chargeable income for the year ended 31 March 2005 will be £150,000.

Required

(a) Compute the chargeable gain which will arise as a result of each of the two proposed disposals. (10 marks)

(b) Advise the directors of ABC Ltd which asset will generate sufficient funds, after taking into account the corporation tax payable on the gain, to allow them to repay the outstanding loan. (5 marks)

Please note that this question does NOT require you to calculate the TOTAL corporation tax payable by ABC Ltd. **(15 marks)**

Assume indexation factors:
May 1989 – May 1996   0.330
June 1997 – December 2004   0.180
May 1990 – December 2004   0.472

56   A LTD

On 1 July 2004 A Ltd, a manufacturing company resident in the United Kingdom, acquired 100% of the share capital of B Ltd, also a manufacturing company. B Ltd makes up accounts each year to 30 June. For its year ended 30 June 2005, it sustained a trading loss of £130,000 and had no other chargeable income. A Ltd produced the following information in relation to its nine-month period of accounts to 31 December 2004.

INCOME	£
Adjusted trading profits	42,000
Rents receivable	13,000
Loan interest receivable (received gross)	8,000
(including £2,000 accrued at 31 December 2004)	
Bank interest receivable (including £3,000	5,000
accrued at 31 December 2004: £2,000 received 30 June 2004)	
Franked investment income (FII)	1,000
(including tax credit received August 2004)	
Charges Paid:	
Gift aid payment (paid September 2004)	17,000

Required

Compute the final taxation position of A Ltd for the above accounting period, assuming maximum group relief is claimed by A Ltd in respect of B Ltd's trading loss.

State the due date for payment of the corporation tax and the date by which A Ltd must file a corporation tax return in respect of the above period.

(15 marks)

57 **MRS DOUGLAS**

(a) Mrs Douglas is the sole shareholder and director of Zeta Ltd. The company is estimated to make a profit of £30,000 in the year to 31 March 2005 (after paying out the salary below). It has no corporation tax liability due to the use of losses from previous years.

Mrs Douglas has received a salary of £4,800 in 2004/05 from the company. She has no other sources of income.

Required

Calculate the net amount of income after tax and national insurance from the company in the hands of Mrs Douglas for 2004/05 if:

(i)   the company pays her a bonus of £10,000 on 1 April 2005; or

(5 marks)

(ii) the company pays her a dividend of £10,000 on 1 April 2005.

(7 marks)

(b) Mrs Douglas has enquired whether it would be more advantageous for her not to receive any salary from Zeta Ltd next year, but simply a dividend of £15,000. The company is likely to make a profit next year and will be liable to corporation tax.

Required

State whether such a course of action would be advantageous. Assume the rates and rules of tax in 2004/05 also apply in 2005/06.   (3 marks)

(15 marks)

58   ROGER AND BRIGITTE

Roger and Brigitte commenced in business on 1 October 2000 as hotel proprietors, sharing profits equally.

On 1 October 2002 their son Xavier joined the partnership and from that date each of the partners was entitled to one-third of the profits.

The profits of the partnership adjusted for income tax, are:

	£
Period ended 30 June 2001	30,000
Year ended 30 June 2002	45,000
Year ended 30 June 2003	50,000
Year ended 30 June 2004	60,000

Required

(a) **Calculate the assessable profits on each of the partners for all relevant years from 2000/01 to 2004/05; and**   (11 marks)

(b) **Calculate the overlap profits for each of the partners.**   (4 marks)

(15 marks)

MOCK EXAM 1: ANSWERS

WARNING! APPLYING OUR MARKING SCHEME

If you decide to mark your paper using our marking scheme, you should bear in mind the following points.

1 The BPP solutions are not definitive: you will see that we have applied the marking scheme to our solutions to show how good answers should gain marks, but there may be more than one way to answer the question. You must try to judge fairly whether different points made in your answers are correct and relevant and therefore worth marks according to our marking scheme.

2 If you have a friend or colleague who is studying or has studied this paper, you might ask him or her to mark your paper for you, thus gaining a more objective assessment. Remember you and your friend are not trained or objective markers, so try to avoid complacency or pessimism if you appear to have done very well or very badly.

3 You should be aware that BPP's answers are longer than you would be expected to write. Sometimes, therefore, you would gain the same number of marks for making the basic point as we have shown as being available for a slightly more detailed or extensive solution.

It is most important that you analyse your solutions in detail and that you attempt to be as objective as possible.

A PLAN OF ATTACK

What's the worst thing you could be doing right now if this was the actual exam paper? Sharpening your pencil? Wondering how to celebrate the end of the exam in 2 hours 59 minutes time? Panicking, flapping and generally getting in a right old state?

Well, they're all pretty bad, so turn back to the paper and let's sort out a **plan of attack**!

First things first

Spend a good 5 minutes looking through the paper in detail working out which optional questions to do and the order in which to attack the questions. You've then got **two options**.

Option 1 (if you're thinking 'Help!')

If you're a bit worried about the paper, do the questions in the order of how well you think you can answer them. You will probably find the optional questions in Section B less daunting than the compulsory questions in Section A so start with Section B.

- The requirements of **question 54** are broken down, which is helpful in allocating your time. Also, you can clearly see where the marks are. If you like VAT and could answer each part of the question this may well have been worth doing. Answer the question in 27 minutes.

- If you are totally happy with chargeable gains calculations then start with **question 55**. If you feel you are doing these computations correctly, it will boost your confidence. However, before you choose a question with two parts like this, ensure you can answer both parts.

- **Question 56** is another mainly computational question. If you are happy with group relief and you like the computations this question could give you another confidence boost. Allow yourself 27 minutes to answer the question and make sure that you state the due dates for easy marks.

- **Question 57** is a tax planning question. This is a fairly standard question and you might have well been advised to do this if you were familiar with this area. Ensure you answer both parts of the question.

- **Question 58** is a fairly straightforward partnership question. If you feel confident with these computations you should have selected this question. You need to set up the correct pro-forma first.

When you've spent the allocated time on the three questions in Section B turn to the compulsory questions in Section A. You should have 1 hour and 30 minutes left at this point in the exam. Read the compulsory questions through thoroughly before you launch into them. Once you start make sure you allocate your time to the parts within the questions according to the marks available and that, where possible, you attempt the easy marks first.

Lastly, what you mustn't forget is that you have to **answer both questions in Section A, and THREE questions from Section B**. Once you've decided on your three questions from Section B, it might be worth putting a line through the other questions so that you are not tempted to answer them!

Option 2 (if you're thinking 'It's a doddle')

It never pays to be over confident but if you're not quaking in your shoes about the exam then **turn straight to the compulsory questions** in Section A. You've got to do them so you might as well get them over and done with.

Once you've done the compulsory questions, choose three of the questions in Section B.

- If you prefer working with numbers rather than providing written answers it might be best to avoid **question 54** in Section B.

- Your choice from the other questions really depends on what you are most confident at. The other questions are all fairly standard computational questions.

No matter how many times we remind you....

Always, always **allocate your time** according to the marks for the question in total and then according to the parts of the question. And **always, always follow the requirements** exactly. Question 52, for example, asks you to explain your reasons for claiming loss relief. So give an explanation.

You've got spare time at the end of the exam.....?

If you have allocated your time properly then you **shouldn't have time on your hands** at the end of the exam. But if you find yourself with five or ten minutes to spare, check over your work to make sure that there are no silly arithmetical errors.

Forget about it!

And don't worry if you found the paper difficult. More than likely other candidates will too. If this were the real thing you would need to **forget** the exam the minute you leave the exam hall and **think about the next one**. Or, if it's the last one, **celebrate**!

52 UNUSUAL URNS LTD

> **Tutor's hint.** The first consideration when relieving losses is the rate at which relief will be obtained. Cash flow is a secondary consideration.

(a) Corporation tax computation

	£
Trading profits	900,000
Less: capital allowances (W1)	(210,750)
industrial buildings allowances (W2)	(3,920)
Schedule D Case I	685,330
Schedule D Case III (£5,000 + £40,000)	45,000
	730,330
Less charge on income paid (gift aid)	(20,000)
Profits chargeable to corporation tax	710,330

	£
FY03 and FY04	
£710,330 × 30%	213,099
Less: small companies' marginal relief 11/400 (1,500,000 – 710,330)	(21,716)
Mainstream corporation tax payable	191,383

As Unusual Urns Ltd is not a 'large' company, the mainstream corporation tax of £191,383 is all due for payment on 1 November 2005.

(b) The loss of £150,000 sustained in the period ended 31 January 2004 could be:

(i)   carried back under s 393A ICTA 1988 to set against the profits before charges arising in the year to 31 July 2003;

(ii) carried forward to set against Schedule D Case I trading profits arising in the year to 31 January 2005.

If the loss is carried forward it will all save tax at the marginal rate of 32.75% in the year to 31 January 2005. There will be no unrelieved charges as a result of the loss relief.

If the loss is carried back tax will be saved only at the small companies rate. Again, there will be no unrelieved charges as a result of the loss relief.

Whichever option is chosen, the gift aid donation in 6 months to 31 January 2004 will be unrelieved.

Despite the cash flow disadvantage of not reliving losses until later, it is recommended that the losses are carried forward as this saves more tax.

Workings

1   *Capital allowances*

	FYA £	Pool £	Short life asset £	Expen- sive car (1) £	Expen- sive car (2) £	Allow- ances £
TWDV b/f		223,000	2,500	16,000		
Additions		60,000			35,000	
Disposals		(60,000)	(500)	(18,000)		
		223,000	2,000	(2,000)	35,000	
WDA @ 25%/ (restricted)		(55,750)			(3,000)	58,750
Balancing allow- ance /charge			(2,000)	2,000		-
Additions	380,000					
FYA @ 40%	(152,000)					152,000
		228,000				210,750
		395,250			32,000	

Note. The company is a medium sized enterprise for capital allowance purposes, so FYAs are due at 40%.

2   *Industrial buildings allowances*

Following the extension of the offices the total expenditure on the administration offices was £40,000. This will not qualify for IBAs in the accounting period to 31 January 2005 as it exceeds 25% of the total expenditure potentially qualifying for IBAs.

Expenditure qualifying for IBAs

	£
Levelling land	2,000
Factory	90,000
Architect's fees	6,000
	98,000

IBAs 4% × £98,000 = £3,920

Marking Guide

		Marks
(a)	Schedule D III	
	– loan interest	1
	– bank interest	1
	Capital allowances	
	– disposals	1
	– additions	1
	– WDAs	1
	– max £3,000 for car	1
	– balancing charge	1
	– balancing allowance	1
	– FYA	2
	Industrial buildings allowance	
	– 2000 costs	1
	– levelling land	1
	– factory	1
	– architect's fees	1
	– exclusion of administration offices	2
	– WDA	1
	Gift aid donation	1
	Calculation of corporation tax	
	– full rate	1
	– small companies' marginal relief	1
	Payment date	2
		22
(b) (i)	Carry back (s 393A(1))	1½
	Carry forward (s 393(1))	1½
(ii)	Deciding factor	2
	Small companies rate to 31.7.03	1
	Marginal rate to 31.1.05	1
	Charges	1
		8
		30

BPP
PROFESSIONAL EDUCATION

53   WILLIAM WISE

> **Tutor's hint**. In our answer we have made notes on why various adjustments were made. This is done for tutorial purposes. You did not need to give the explanations in the exam as they were not asked for. Always read the question.

(a)

	£	£
Net profit		30,200
Add: Depreciation	4,760	
Private light and heat (40%)	610	
Private motor expenses (75%)	3,540	
Legal fees	1,200	
Personal tax	250	
Private rent and rates (40%)	1,560	
Repairs and renewals	1,050	
Food hampers	640	
Donation	100	
Wife's salary (excessive amount)	4,500	
Goods for own use	650	
		18,860
Less: Capital allowances (W1)		(13,060)
Schedule D Case I profit		36,000

Notes

1   The legal fees incurred in connection with the clothing shop are not allowable since they relate to a capital item.

2   Personal or private expenses are not allowable.

3   The £2,200 spent on repairs in May 2004 is allowable because the shop was in a fit state to use on purchase.

4   Gifts of **food** are not allowable. However, the gifts of pens are allowable because the pens carry a conspicuous advertisement for the business and cost less than £50 each.

5   A donation to a national charity is not allowable. The donation to the local charity can be allowed as it carried an advertisement for the business and could be said to be made for the purposes of the trade.

6   Goods taken for own use must be brought into the profit and loss account at selling price.

7   The excessive part of William's wife's salary is not allowable.

Workings

1   *Capital allowances*

	FYA @ 50% £	*General pool* £	*Private use car* £	*Allow- ances* £
Addition			14,000	
WDA (restricted)			(3,000) × 25%	750
			11,000	
Fixtures	19,520			
FYA @ 50%	(9,760)			9,760
		9,760		
Computer	5,100			
FYA @ 50%	(2,550)	2,550		2,550
		-		
		12,310	11,000	13,060

(b)

	Non- savings income £	*Dividend income* £	*Allow- ance* £
Schedule D Case I (1.6.04 – 5.4.05)			
(10/12 × £36,000)	30,000		
Dividends (× 100/90)		7,500	
STI	30,000	7,500	£37,500
Less: personal allowance	(4,745)		
	25,255	7,500	£32,755

	£
Tax on non-savings income	
£2,020 × 10%	202
£23,235 × 22%	5,112
Tax on dividend income	
£6,145 × 10%	615
£1,355 × 32.5%	440
	6,369

Class 4 NICs:

(£30,000 – £4,745) ×8%	£2,020

(c) (i)   William can base a personal pension contribution for 2004/05 on his earnings for 2004/05, or on his earnings for any of the five previous tax years.

The maximum contribution for 2004/05 is therefore:

20% × £48,000 = £9,600

(ii)   This contribution must be paid by 31.1.06.

(iii) A personal pension contribution is paid net of basic rate tax. Additional relief is given in the personal tax computation by extending the basic rate band by the gross amount of the contribution.

Marking guide

		Marks
(a)	Net profit	½
	Depreciation	1
	Private use of light/heat	1
	Private motor expenses	1
	Legal fees	1
	Personal tax	1
	Private rent/rates	1
	Repairs/renewals	1
	Food hampers	1
	Donation	1
	Wife's salary	1
	Goods for own use	1
	Capital allowances	2½
		14
(b)	Taxable income	2
	Income tax	2
	Class 4 NICs	1
		5
(c)	Basis years	1
	Max contribution	2
	Payment date	1
	Paid net of BRT	1
	Extend basic rate band	1
		6
		25

54   REGISTRATION, ERRORS AND DEREGISTRATION

> **Tutor's hint**. It was important to ensure that you allocated your time properly between the various parts in this question.

(a) (i) **Training**

Confused Ltd will be required to register for VAT as it will be making taxable supplies in excess of the registration threshold.

Output tax	£
Sales (£75,000 × 17½%)	13,125
Less: input tax (£10,000 × 7/47)	(1,489)
VAT due	11,636

(ii) **Transport**

Confused Ltd will be required to notify Customs of a need to register for VAT but because it is making only zero-rated supplies it may ask custom's permission not to register for VAT. The advantage of registration is that input VAT of £1,489 per month will be reclaimable.

	£
Output tax	NIL
Less: input tax	(1,489)
VAT repayment due	(1,489)

(iii) **Air ambulance services**

If exempt supplies only are made the company will not be permitted to register for VAT. No VAT will be due or reclaimable.

(b) **Errors on a VAT return of up to £2,000** (net under declaration minus over declaration) **may be corrected on the next VAT return without giving rise to either a misdeclaration penalty** or default interest.

Other errors may be voluntarily disclosed separately to Customs & Excise. Default interest and, in certain circumstances, the misdeclaration penalty, will apply in respect of these errors.

(c) On **cessation of the trade**, Perplexed Ltd **will have to deregister for VAT.** On deregistration **VAT will be due on all assets sold on a piecemeal basis in respect of which input VAT was claimed. If the VAT chargeable does not exceed £1,000,** it need **not be paid.**

The company will need to **notify Customs within 30 days of the cessation of trade.**

If the business is **sold as a going concern, no VAT is due as a sale of a going concern is outside the scope** of VAT. The purchaser will need to register for VAT. The purchaser can take over Perplexed Ltd's VAT registration if it wishes. Otherwise, the old registration is cancelled.

55   **ABC LTD**

> **Tutor's hint**. The question emphasised that you were not required to calculate the total corporation tax payable by ABC Ltd. You would not have gained any marks for doing so.

(a)   **Gain on disposal of land in May 1996**

	£
Sale proceeds in May 1996	140,000
Less cost	(80,000)
	60,000
Less: Indexation allowance = 0.330 × £80,000	(26,400)
	33,600
Gain rolled over (£33,600 – £10,000)	(23,600)
Proceeds retained (£140,000 – £130,000)	10,000

Sale of land

	£	£
Sale proceeds		700,000
Less : Cost	130,000	
Less: gain rolled	(23,600)	
		(106,400)
		593,600
Less: Indexation allowance = 0.180 × £106,400		(19,152)
Chargeable gain		574,448

DEF Ltd shares

	£
Proceeds	700,000
Less cost	(40,000)
	660,000
Less: indexation allowance 0.472 × £40,000	(18,880)
	641,120

(b)   **Funds for loan repayment**

As ABC Ltd and DEF Ltd are associated companies, the small companies rate thresholds are divided by two, giving upper and lower limits for small companies rate purposes of £750,000 and £150,000 respectively. Because of the other chargeable income of £150,000 for the year ended 31 March 2005, the chargeable gains will bear corporation tax at the marginal rates of 32.75% on £600,000 and 30% on any excess.

	Plot of land £	DEF Ltd Shares £
Proceeds	700,000	700,000
Corporation tax at marginal rate of 32.75%	(188,132)	(196,500)
Corporation tax at marginal rate of 30%		(12,336)
Net sale proceeds	511,868	491,164

The directors need approximately £510,000 in order to repay the loan, so only the sale of the land generates sufficient net sale proceeds to repay the loan.

They should be advised to sell the plot of land rather then the shares, since this generates more net cash after taking into account the corporation tax that must be paid on the chargeable gain.

In addition, if either ABC Ltd or DEF Ltd buys further capital assets qualifying for rollover relief within the next three years, the gain arising on the sale of the land can once more be deferred through rollover relief.

Marking guide

		Marks	
(a)	Gain in May 1996 (amount to rollover)	3	
	Gain on sale of land December 2004	4	
	Gain on sale of shares December 2004	3	
			10
(b)	Dividing of limits	1	
	Net sale proceeds	3	
	Advice	1	
			5
			15

56 A LTD

Tutor's hint. B Ltd's loss could be set only against the available profits of the corresponding accounting period.

Corporation Tax computation

	£	£
Schedule D Case I		42,000
Schedule A		13,000
Schedule D Case III		
Bank interest accrued	5,000	
Loan interest accrued	8,000	
		13,000
		68,000
Less: charges on income:		
Gift aid		(17,000)
		51,000
Less: group relief (W1)		(34,000)
PCTCT		17,000
Add: Franked Investment Income		1,000
'Profits'		18,000

	£
Corporation tax	
FY2004	
£17,000 × 19%	3,230
Less: starting rate marginal relief	
$19/400 (£18,750 - 18,000) \times \frac{17,000}{18,000}$	(34)
Mainstream corporation tax	3,196

£3,196 must be paid by 1 October 2005.

The corporation tax return for the period must be filed by 31 December 2005.

Notes

It is assumed that the loan interest and the bank interest arose on non-trading loans and is therefore taxable under Schedule D Case III.

Workings

1   B Ltd joined the group with A Ltd on 1 July 2004 so for A Ltd's profit making accounting period to 31 December 2004 there are 6 months in common with B Ltd's loss making period.

Thus

A Ltd	6/9 □ £51,000	= £34,000
B Ltd	6/12 □ (£130,000)	= £65,000

Maximum group relief available is lower of two, ie £34,000.

2   The 9 months to 31 December 2004 falls into FY2004.

'Profits' are between the starting rate upper and lower limits of £50,000 × 9/12 ÷ 2 = £18,750 and £10,000 × 9/12 ÷ 2 = £3,750, so the starting rate marginal relief applies.

Marking guide	
	Marks
Schedule DI	½
Schedule A	½
Schedule DIII	2
Gift aid	1
Group relief	5
FII	1
CT calculation	3
Due dates	2
	15

57   **MRS DOUGLAS**

> **Tutor's hint.** A combination of remuneration and dividends is usually best.

(a) (i)   **Bonus**

Income tax 2004/05

	Non savings income £	Total £
Salary	4,800	
Bonus	10,000	
STI	14,800	14,800
Less: PA	(4,745)	
Taxable income	10,055	10,055

Tax

	£
£2,020 × 10%	202
£8,035 (10,055 – 2,020) × 22%	1,768
	1,970

National insurance – Class 1	
£ (14,800 – 4,745) × 11% =	£1,106

Net income after tax and NICs	
£(14,800 – 1,970 – 1,106) =	£11,724

(ii)

	Non savings income £	Dividend income £	Total £
Salary	4,800		
Dividend £10,000 × 100/90		11,111	
STI	4,800	11,111	15,911
Less: PA	(4,745)		
Taxable income	55	11,111	11,166

Tax

	£
£55 × 10%	6
£11,111 × 10%	1,111
	1,117
Less: tax credit on dividend	(1,111)
Tax liability	6

National insurance – Class 1	
£55 (4,800 – 4,745) × 11% =	6

Net income after tax and NICs	
£(4,800 + 10,000 – 6 – 6) =	14,788

(b) **A combination of dividends and remuneration usually gives the best result.**

Remuneration and the cost of benefits are allowed as deductions in computing the company's profits chargeable to corporation tax. This could affect the rate of corporation tax. If the company profits in the year to 1 April 2005 are below £50,000 and a dividend is paid to Mrs Douglas additional corporation tax will be due. The amount of the dividend will be assessed to corporation tax at 19% and will not qualify for either the 0% rate or starting rate marginal relief.

A certain minimum amount of salary should be paid out to protect National Insurance benefits and also to use the personal allowance. If the PA was set against the dividend income, it would simply restrict the tax credit available and not result in any repayment of tax.

Marking guide

		Marks	
(a) (i)	Salary and bonus	1	
	Personal Allowance	½	
	Tax calculation	1	
	NIC calculation	1½	
	Net income after tax	<u>1</u>	
			5
(ii)	Salary and dividend	2	
	Personal allowance	½	
	Tax calculation	1	
	Tax credit	1	
	NIC calculation	1½	
	Net income after tax	<u>1</u>	
			7
(b)	Combination of salary/divis	1	
	Impact for company	1	
	NI benefits	<u>1</u>	
			<u>3</u>
			<u><u>15</u></u>

58   ROGER AND BRIGITTE

> **Tutor's hint.** First allocate the profits of each accounting period between the partners.

(a)   The profits of each partner are as follows.

	Total £	Roger £	Brigitte £	Xavier £
1.10.00 – 30.6.01		30,000	15,000	15,000	
1.7.01 – 30.6.02		45,000	22,500	22,500	
1.7.02 – 30.6.03					
1.7.02 – 30.9.02 (3/12)	12,500		6,250	6,250	
1.10.02 – 30.6.03 (9/12)	37,500		12,500	12,500	12,500
		50,000	18,750	18,750	12,500
1.7.03 – 30.6.04		60,000	20,000	20,000	20,000

The assessable profits for the tax years are, therefore, as follows.

	Roger £	Brigitte £	Xavier £
2000/01			
(1.10.00 – 5.4.01)			
£15,000 × 6/9	10,000	10,000	–
2001/02			
(1.10.00 – 30.9.01)			
£15,000 + (£22,500 × 3/12)	20,625	20,625	–
2002/03			
(1.7.01 – 30.6.02)	22,500	22,500	
(1.10.02 – 5.4.03)			
£12,500 × 6/9			8,333
2003/04			
(1.7.02 – 30.6.03)	18,750	18,750	
(1.10.02 – 30.9.03)			
£12,500 + 3/12 × £20,000			17,500
2004/05			
(1.7.03 – 30.6.04)	20,000	20,000	20,000

(b)   The overlap profits for both Roger and Brigitte are:

	Profits £
1.10.00 – 5.4.01	10,000
1.7.01 – 30.9.01	5,625
	15,625

Xavier's overlap profits are:

	£
1.10.02 – 5.4.03	8,333
1.7.03 – 30.9.03	5,000
	13,333

Marking Guide

	Marks
Apportionment of profits	
- period 30.6.01	1
- y/end 30.6.02	1
- y/end 30.6.03	2
- y/end 30.6.04	1
Assessable profits	
00/01	1
01/02	1
02/03	1
03/04	2
04/05	1
	11
Overlap profits	
Roger	1
Brigitte	1
Xavier	2
	4
	15

Business Taxation
Mock Exam 2

Question Paper:	
Time allowed	**3 hours**
Section A	**BOTH questions MUST be answered**

paper 2.3

SECTION A – BOTH questions are compulsory and MUST be attempted.

59   UNFORESEEN UPSETS LIMITED

Unforeseen Upsets Limited (UUL) is a United Kingdom resident company which has been manufacturing lifeboats for many years. It has no associated companies. The company has previously made up accounts to 31 December but has now changed its accounting date to 31 March.

The company's results for the 15 month period to 31 March 2005 are as follows.

	£
Trading profits (as adjusted for taxation but before capital allowances)	1,125,000
Bank interest receivable (note 4)	20,000
Debenture interest receivable (note 5)	17,500
Chargeable gain (notes 6 and 7)	30,000
Gift aid donation paid (note 8)	20,000
Dividends received from UK companies (note 9)	6,300

Notes

1   UUL is a small company with a turnover in the period of account ended 31 March 2005 of £2,000,000. The company has 30 employees.

2   *Capital allowances – plant and machinery*

On 1 January 2004 the tax written-down values of plant and machinery were:

	£
Pool	142,000

Sales during the accounting period were:

		£
31.7.04	3 cars (not low emission)	15,000
30.9.04	Plant and machinery	12,000

Additions during the accounting period were:

		£
1.6.04	1 car (not low emission)	14,000
1.8.04	3 cars (£8,000 each) (not low emission)	24,000
30.11.04	Plant and machinery	92,000
28.2.05	Computer equipment	2,400

3   On 1 January 2004 the company had trading losses brought forward of £600,000.

4   *Bank interest receivable*

	£
31.3.04 received	3,000
30.6.04 received	4,000
30.9.04 received	5,000
31.12.04 received	8,000
	20,000

All interest was received at the end of the quarter for which accrued. The bank interest was non trading income.

5 . *Debenture interest receivable (gross amounts)*

	£
30.9.04 received	10,500
31.3.05 received	7,000
	17,500

(a) The loan was made on 1 July 2004.

(b) £1,500 was accrued at 31 December 2004. There was no accrual at 31 March 2005.

(c) The interest was non-trading income.

(d) The interest was received gross from another UK company.

6 The chargeable gain was realised on 1 July 2004.

7 On 1 January 2004 the company had capital losses brought forward of £50,000.

8 *Gift aid donations paid*

	£
31.5.04	7,000
31.10.04	4,000
28.2.05	9,000
	20,000

9 *Dividends received*

28.2.05	£6,300

Required

(a) **Calculate the mainstream corporation tax payable for the fifteen month period of account.** (20 marks)

(b) **State the date(s) by which the company must pay its mainstream corporation tax liability, the date by which it must file return(s) and the penalties due if returns are not filed by the due date.** (9 marks)

(c) **State what unrelieved amounts are carried forward at 31 March 2005.**
(1 mark)

(30 marks)

60   MARIO AND MARISA

Mario and Marisa married in 1988. Mario is now 45 and Marisa is 42.

In 2004/05 Mario received a salary from his employer of £27,749. Mario was provided with a company car by his employer. Until 5 September 2004 he had the use of a petrol car whose list price was £10,500 which had a CO_2 emissions figure of 146g/km. On 6 September 2004 the car was changed for a new diesel car with a list price of £16,000. The diesel car had a CO_2 emissions figure of 184/km.

All fuel was paid for by his employer.

On 6 October 2003 Mario was provided with a computer for both business and private use at home. The computer cost Mario's employer £3,000 on 6 October 2003.

Mario received bank interest from Lloyds Bank of £120 on 30 June 2004.

Mario and Marisa moved into a new home on 6 April 2004. The purchase of the house was funded by a loan of £20,000 from Mario's employer on which annual interest of 2% was payable.

Marisa has made a capital gain in 2004/05. The gain arose on the disposal of a business asset that had been owned since August 1995. The cost of the asset was

£13,825 and the proceeds were £73,000. The indexation allowance from August 1995 to April 1998 was £1,175.

Marisa has carried on a garment manufacturing business since June 1998. She makes up annual accounts to 31 March. The adjusted trading profit before capital allowances to 31 March 2005 was £49,500 and the capital allowances on plant and machinery were £2,500. On 1 April 2002 she purchased a new factory for £100,000 which was immediately brought into use. On 30 September 2004 Marisa sold the factory for £55,000. The factory was always used in the business.

Required

Calculate the tax liabilities for the year 2004/05 of:

(a) Mario; and	(13 marks)
(b) Marisa	(12 marks)

Assume that the official rate of interest is 5%.   **(25 marks)**

61   DEFAULT SURCHARGE, CASH ACCOUNTING

Vector Ltd is registered for VAT, and is in the process of completing its VAT return for the quarter ended 31 March 2005. The following information is available.

(1) Sales invoices totalling £128,000 were issued in respect of standard rated sales. Vector Ltd offers its customers a 2.5% discount for prompt payment.

(2) On 15 March 2005 Vector Ltd received an advance deposit of £4,500 in respect of a contract that is due to be completed during April 2005. The total value of the contract is £10,000.

(3) Standard rated expenses amounted to £74,800. This includes £4,200 for entertaining customers.

(4) On 31 March 2005 Vector Ltd wrote off £12,000 due from a customer as a bad debt. The debt was in respect of three invoices, each of £4,000, that were due for payment on 15 August, 15 September and 15 October 2004 respectively.

(5) On 1 January 2005 the company purchased a motor car costing £9,800 for the use of its sales manager. The sales manager is provided with free petrol for private mileage. The relevant quarterly scale charge is £432. Both figures are inclusive of VAT.

Unless stated otherwise all of the above figures are exclusive of VAT.

For the quarter ended 31 December 2004 Vector Ltd was one month late in submitting its VAT return and in paying the related VAT liability.

Required

(a) Calculate the amount of VAT payable by Vector Ltd for the quarter ended 31 March 2005.   (7 marks)

(b) Explain the implications if for the quarter ended 31 March 2005 Vector Ltd is one month late in submitting its VAT return and in paying the related VAT liability   (3 marks)

(c) State the conditions that Vector Ltd must satisfy before it will be permitted to use the cash accounting scheme, and advise the company of the implications of using the scheme.   (5 marks)

                                                                              (15 marks)

62 CHANDRA KHAN

Chandra Khan disposed of the following assets during 2004/05:

(a) On 15 June 2004 Chandra sold 10,000 £1 ordinary shares (a 30% shareholding) in Universal Ltd, an unquoted trading company, to her daughter for £75,000. The market value of the shares on this date was £110,000. The shareholding was purchased on 10 July 2000 for £38,000. Chandra and her daughter have elected to hold over the gain as a gift of a business asset.

(b) On 8 November 2004 Chandra sold a freehold factory for £146,000. The factory was purchased on 3 January 1997 for £72,000. 75% of the factory has been used in a manufacturing business run by Chandra as a sole trader. However, the remaining 25% of the factory has never been used for business purposes. Chandra has claimed to rollover the gain on the factory against the replacement cost of a new freehold factory that was purchased on 10 November 2004 for £156,000. The new factory is used 100% for business purposes by Chandra.

(c) On 8 March 2005 Chandra incorporated a wholesale business that she has run as a sole trader since 1 May 2003. The market value of the business on 8 March 2005 was £250,000. All of the business assets were transferred to a new limited company, with the consideration consisting of 200,000 £1 ordinary shares valued at £200,000 and £50,000 in cash. The only chargeable asset of the business was goodwill, and this was valued at £100,000 on 8 March 2005. The goodwill has a nil cost.

Required

Calculate the capital gains arising from Chandra's disposals during 2004–05. You should ignore the indexation allowance and the annual exemption.

Each of the three sections of this question carries equal marks (five marks each). **(15 marks)**

63 MR K

Mr K is the managing director of Q Ltd. The company provides him with a number of benefits in addition to his salary of £60,000 per annum.

For 2004/05 these benefits comprise:

(a) *Motor cars*

Mr K was given the use of a Mercedes car which had cost the company £24,000 and had CO_2 emissions of 147g/km. On 5 August 2004, Mr K was involved in a serious accident in which the Mercedes was totally destroyed. Mr K was injured and did not drive or return to work until 5 October 2004.

On his return to work on 5 October 2004, he was provided with a Lexus motor car which cost the company £36,000. The CO_2 emissions of the car are 197g/km.

As a result of the car crash, Mr K was found guilty of dangerous driving and the company paid his legal costs and fine amounting to £1,200 with Mr K making a contribution of £300.

Mr K was provided with petrol for both cars by the company, including that used for private mileage.

(b) *Suits*

Mr K was provided, for the whole of the tax year, with two suits of clothes, each costing £800.

(c) *Housing*

Mr K lived in a house owned by the company, which bought it last year for £125,000. The annual rental value was £8,000 and Mr K paid rent of £5,000 to the company.

The company is currently considering, for the first time, paying annual cash bonuses to its directors.

Required

(a) **Compute the total value of the benefits assessable on Mr K for the year 2004/05. Assume the official rate of interest is 5%.** (7 marks)

(b) **Compute any additional cost to be met by the company as a result of providing the above benefits.** (1 mark)

(c) **Draft a short memo to the board explaining the method of taxing bonuses paid to directors and indicating how the tax will be accounted for.** (7 marks)

(15 marks)

64 STRAIGHT PLC

Straight plc is the holding company for a group of companies. All of the companies in the group have an accounting date of 31 March. The group structure is as follows:

Straight plc

|

100%

|

Arc Ltd

|

80%

|

Bend Ltd

|

75%

|

Curve Ltd

For the year ended 31 March 2005 Straight plc has a Schedule DI trading profit of £185,000. As at 31 March 2004 the company had unused trading losses of £15,000 and unused capital losses of £10,000.

Straight plc sold a freehold office building on 20 June 2004 for £350,000, and this resulted in a capital gain of £140,000. The company has made a rollover relief claim in respect of a replacement building purchased for £270,000.

During the year ended 31 March 2005 Straight plc received dividends of £18,000 from Arc Ltd, and dividends of £9,000 from Triangle plc, an unconnected company. These figures are the actual amounts received.

Arc Ltd sold a freehold warehouse on 10 March 2005, and this resulted in a capital loss of £40,000.

Required

(a) Explain why Straight plc, Arc Ltd, Bend Ltd and Curve Ltd form a group for capital gains purposes, and why Curve Ltd would be excluded from the group if Straight plc's holding in Arc Ltd were only 80% instead of 100%. (4 marks)

(b) Before taking into account any notional transfer of assets, calculate the corporation tax payable by Straight plc for the year ended 31 March 2005. (8 marks)

(c) State the time limit for Straight plc and Arc Ltd to make a joint election so that Straight plc is treated as disposing of Arc Ltd's freehold warehouse, and explain why such an election will be beneficial. You are not expected to consider any alternative joint elections. (3 marks)

(15 marks)

65   **PETER, QUINTON AND ROGER**

Peter and Quinton commenced in partnership on 1 January 2002. Roger joined as a partner on 1 January 2003, and Peter resigned as a partner on 31 December 2004. Profits and losses have always been shared equally. The partnership's Schedule DI profits and losses are as follows:

	£	
Year ended 31 December 2002	40,000	Profit
Year ended 31 December 2003	90,000	Profit
Year ended 31 December 2004	(30,000)	Loss

All of the partners were in employment prior to becoming partners, and each of them has investment income. None of the partners has any capital gains.

Required

(a) Briefly explain the basis by which partners are assessed under Schedule DI or DII when they join a partnership. (2 marks)

(b) Calculate the Schedule DI assessments of Peter, Quinton and Roger for 2001/02, 2002/03 and 2003/04. (6 marks)

(c) State the possible ways in which Peter, Quinton and Roger can relieve their share of the Schedule DI trading loss for 2004/05. Your answer should include a calculation of the amount of loss relief available to each partner. (7 marks)

(15 marks)

MOCK EXAM 2: ANSWERS

**DO NOT TURN THIS PAGE UNTIL YOU
HAVE COMPLETED THE MOCK EXAM**

WARNING! APPLYING OUR MARKING SCHEME

If you decide to mark your paper using our marking scheme, you should bear in mind the following points.

1   The BPP solutions are not definitive: you will see that we have applied the marking scheme to our solutions to show how good answers should gain marks, but there may be more than one way to answer the question. You must try to judge fairly whether different points made in your answers are correct and relevant and therefore worth marks according to our marking scheme.

2   If you have a friend or colleague who is studying or has studied this paper, you might ask him or her to mark your paper for you, thus gaining a more objective assessment. Remember you and your friend are not trained or objective markers, so try to avoid complacency or pessimism if you appear to have done very well or very badly.

3   You should be aware that BPP's answers are longer than you would be expected to write. Sometimes, therefore, you would gain the same number of marks for making the basic point as we have shown as being available for a slightly more detailed or extensive solution.

It is most important that you analyse your solutions in detail and that you attempt to be as objective as possible.

A PLAN OF ATTACK

What's the worst thing you could be doing right now if this was the actual exam paper? Sharpening your pencil? Wondering how to celebrate the end of the exam in 2 hours 59 minutes time? Panicking, flapping and generally getting in a right old state?

Well, they're all pretty bad, so turn back to the paper and let's sort out a **plan of attack**!

First things first

Spend a good 5 minutes looking through the paper in detail working out which optional questions to do and the order in which to attack the questions. You've then got **two options**.

Option 1 (if you're thinking 'Help!')

If you're a bit worried about the paper, do the questions in the order of how well you think you can answer them. You will probably find the optional questions in Section B less daunting than the compulsory questions in Section A so start with Section B.

- **Question 61** deals with various aspects of VAT. If you like VAT and could answer each part of the question this may well have been worth doing, as it could be done quickly. But if you are hazy on these areas you should not answer this question as you would need to be very accurate to gain good marks.

- If you like chargeable gains, **question 62** would be a good choice. Make sure you can do all the parts before you pick this one to do.

- **Question 63** contains three parts. Part (c) is written and so if you don't like written questions this might have been best avoided.

- **Question 64** is a question about groups. If you are happy with the different types of groups and their corresponding reliefs then this question could give you a confidence boost.

- **Question 65** is mainly computational. If you feel confident with the computations involved with partnerships this might be a good question to do.

When you've spent the allocated time on the three questions in Section B turn to the compulsory questions in Section A. You should have 1 hour and 30 minutes left at this point in the exam. Read the compulsory questions through thoroughly before you launch into them. Once you start make sure you allocate your time to the parts within the questions according to the marks available and that, where possible, you attempt the easy marks first.

Lastly, what you mustn't forget is that you have to **answer both questions in Section A, and THREE questions from Section B**. Once you've decided on your three questions from Section B, it might be worth putting a line through the other questions so that you are not tempted to answer them!

Option 2 (if you're thinking 'It's a doddle')

It never pays to be over confident but if you're not quaking in your shoes about the exam then **turn straight to the compulsory questions** in Section A. You've got to do them so you might as well get them over and done with.

Once you've done the compulsory questions, choose three of the questions in Section B.

- If you prefer working with numbers rather than providing written answers it might be best to avoid **question 63** in Section B.

- Your choice from the other questions really depends on what you are most confident at. The other questions are all fairly standard computational questions except **question 61** on VAT, which is on a specialist area.

No matter how many times we remind you....

Always, always **allocate your time** according to the marks for the question in total and then according to the parts of the question. And **always, always follow the requirements** exactly. **Question 64**, for example, asks you to consider five specific headings. You will not gain marks for considering anything else and you will lose marks if you ignore any of the five headings outlined.

You've got spare time at the end of the exam.....?

If you have allocated your time properly then you **shouldn't have time on your hands** at the end of the exam. But if you find yourself with five or ten minutes to spare, check over your work to make sure that there are no silly arithmetical errors.

Forget about it!

And don't worry if you found the paper difficult. More than likely other candidates will too. If this were the real thing you would need to **forget** the exam the minute you leave the exam hall and **think about the next one**. Or, if it's the last one, **celebrate**!

59   UNFORESEEN UPSETS LIMITED

> **Tutor's hint.** Break a long question like this down into manageable parts in order to gain the easy marks. It is essential that you are aware that a long period of account is split into two accounting periods and that the first period is always twelve months in length. If you do not make this split correctly you cannot hope to pass the question.

(a) **Corporation tax computations**

	Year to 31.12.04 £	3 months to 31.3.05 £
Trading profits	900,000	225,000
Less: capital allowances (W1)	(83,750)	(11,279)
	816,250	213,721
Less: losses b/f	(600,000)	
	216,250	213,721
Schedule D Case III (W2)	32,000	5,500
Chargeable gains (W3)	–	–
	248,250	219,221
Less: charges paid	(11,000)	(9,000)
PCTCT	237,250	210,221
Dividends plus tax credits £6,300 × 100/90	–	7,000
'Profits' for small companies rate purposes	237,250	217,221

Corporation tax (W4)

	£	£
FY03 and FY04		
£237,250 × 19%	45,078	
FY04		
£210,221 × 30%		63,066
Less: Small companies marginal relief		
11/400 (£375,000 – £217,221) × $\frac{210,221}{217,221}$		(4,200)
	45,078	58,866

(b) £45,078 in respect of the 12 months to 31 December 2004 must be paid by 1 October 2005.

£58,866 in respect of the 3 months to 31 March 2005 must be paid by 1 January 2006.

A return for the 12 months to 31 December 2004 and a return for the 3 months to 31 March 2005 must be filed by 31 March 2006.

If a return is filed late there is an initial penalty of £100. This rises to £200 if the return is more than 3 months late. These penalties rise to £500 and £1,000 respectively for the third consecutive late filing of a return.

There is in addition a tax geared penalty, if the return is more than six months late. The penalty is 10% of the tax unpaid six months after the return was due if the total delay is up to 12 months, but it increases to 20% of that tax if the return is over 12 months late.

(c) At 31 March 2005 there are capital losses to carry forward of £20,000 (W3).

Workings

1   *Capital allowances*

	FYA £	Pool £	Expensive Car £	Allowances £
Year to 31.12.04				
TWDV b/f		142,000		
Additions		24,000	14,000	
Disposals		(27,000)		
		139,000	14,000	
WDA @ 25%/(restricted)		(34,750)	(3,000)	37,750
Additions	92,000			
FYA @ 50%	(46,000)			46,000
		46,000		83,750
TWDV c/f		150,250	11,000	
3 months to 31.3.05				
WDA @ 25%/(restricted)				
× 3/12		(9,391)	(688)	10,079
Additions	2,400			
FYA @ 50%	(1,200)			1,200
		1,200		11,279
		142,059	10,312	

Note. As Unforeseen Upsets Ltd is **a small enterprise it is entitled to FYAs of 50% on the computer equipment, the plant and machinery**.

2   *Schedule D Case III*

The interest is taxable under Schedule D Case III on an accruals basis:

	Year to 31.12.04 £	3 months to 31.3.05 £
Bank interest	20,000	–
Debenture interest	12,000	5,500
	32,000	5,500

3   *Chargeable gains*

	Year to 31.12.03 £
Gain	30,000
Loss/b/f	(30,000)
Net gain	-

The loss c/f on 1 April 2005 is £20,000 (£50,000 – £30,000).

4   *Corporation tax*

Year to 31 December 2004

The year to 31 December 2004 straddles FY03 and FY04. The rates and limits for these financial years are the same therefore there is no need to apportion the PCTCT or 'profits'. The small companies limit for both years is £300,000, so the small companies rate of 19% applies

3 months to 31 March 2005

	FY04 (3/12) £
Profits	217,221
PCTCT	210,221
Lower limit for small companies rate	75,000
Upper limit for small companies rate	375,000

Small companies marginal relief applies.

Marking guide

		Marks
(a)	Trading profits (12:3)	1
	Trading losses brought forward	1
	Bank interest	1
	Debenture interest	1½
	Chargeable gains (W3)	1½
	Charges paid – Gift Aid Donations	1
	Capital allowances (W1)	
	Year to 31.12.04	
	Sales and additions	1
	WDA	1
	FYA	1
	Period to 31.3.05	
	WDA	1
	FYA	1
	Year to 31.12.04	
	Small companies rate	1
	Tax calculation	2
	Period to 31.3.05	
	Calculation of 'P'	1
	Calculation of reduced limits	1
	Marginal relief	1
	Calculation of liability	2
		20
(b)	Due dates for payment	2
	Due dates for returns	2
	Penalties	5
		9
(c)	Capital losses c/fwd	1
		30

60   MARIO AND MARISA

Tutor's hint. The first £500 of any benefit arising in respect of the private use of computer equipment is exempt.

(a) **Mario - income tax liability**

	Non-savings £	Savings (excl dividend £	Total £
Employment income (W1)	34,438	0	
Bank interest (£120 × 100/80)		150	
Statutory total income	34,438	150	34,588
Less: Personal allowance	(4,745)		
	29,693	150	29,843

Income tax on non-savings income

	£
£2,020 × 10%	202
£27,673 × 22%	6,088

Income tax on savings (excl dividend) income

	£
£150 × 20%	30
Income tax liability	6,320

(b) **Marisa - income tax liability**

	£
Schedule D Case I (£49,500 – £2,500 – 37,000 (W2))	10,000
Less: Personal allowance	(4,745)
Taxable income	5,255

	£
Income tax on non-savings income	
£2,020 × 10%	202
£3,235 × 22%	712
Income tax liability	914

Capital gains tax liability

	£
Gains after taper relief (25%) (W3)	14,500
Less: annual exemption	(8,200)
	6,800

£6,300 × 20% = £1,260.

Workings

1   *Employment income*

	£
Salary	27,749
Car benefit	
Car 1 (£10,500 × 15%) × 5/12	656
Car 2 (£16,000 × 25%) × 7/12	2,333
Fuel benefit	
Car 1 £14,400 × 15% × 5/12	900
Car 2 £14,400 × 25% × 7/12	2,100
Computer equipment (£3,000 × 20% - £500)	100
Taxable cheap loan (£20,000 × 5% – 2%)	600
	34,438

Note. The taxable percentage for the diesel car is calculated by rounding down the CO_2 emission figure to 180/km. The % of 15% is then increased by 1% for each 5g/km that CO_2 emissions exceed 145g/km. 3% is added because the car is a diesel car.

2   *Industrial buildings allowance*

	£
Cost	100,000
WDA at 4%	
y/e 31.3.03	(4,000)
y/e 31.3.04	(4,000)
Residue before sale	92,000

Balancing allowance

	£
Residue before sale	92,000
Less: proceeds	(55,000)
Balancing allowance	37,000

3   *Capital gain*

	£
Proceeds	73,000
Less: cost	(13,825)
Unindexed gain	59,175
Less: indexation allowance	(1,175)
Indexed gain	58,000
Gain after taper relief (25%)	£14,500

Marking guide

			Marks
(a)	(i)	Bank interest	1
		Income tax calculation	2
			3
(b)	(i)	Schedule D Case I	2
		Income tax calculation	1
	(ii)	Taper relief	1
		Annual exemption	1
		Capital gains tax calculation	2
		Tax	1
			8

Employment income (W1)

	Marks
Car 1	
Taxable percentage	1½
Time reduction	1
Car 2	
Taxable percentage	2½
Time reduction	1
Fuel benefits	
Car 1	1
Car 2	1
Computer equipment	1
Beneficial loan	1
	10

IBAs (W2)

	Marks
Allowances claimed	2
Balancing allowance	2
	4
	25

61   DEFAULT SURCHARGE, CASH ACCOUNTING

Tutor's hints. When there are three distinct parts to a question ensure that you allocate your time carefully to each part. In this question you could have attempted the parts in any order, depending on which parts you found easiest.

(a)

	£
Output tax	
Sales (£128,000 × 97.5% × 17.5%)	21,840
Advance payment (£4,500 × 7/47)	670
Petrol scale charge (£432 × 7/47)	64
Input tax	
Standard rated expenses (£74,800 – £4,200) × 17½%	(12,355)
Bad debts (£8,000 × 17½%)	(1,400)
	8,819

Tutorial notes

1   For VAT purposes, assume a prompt payment discount is taken, even if it is not actually taken.

2   The advance payment is assumed to be VAT inclusive.

3   VAT cannot be reclaimed if it relates to the motor car or business entertaining.

4   Relief cannot be given for VAT on the bad debts until at least six months have elapsed from when payment is due.

(b) **A default surcharge liability notice will have been issued following the late submission of the VAT return** for the quarter ended 31 December 2004. There will be a surcharge period running to 31 December 2005.

If the VAT return is late in the quarter to 31 March 2005, a surcharge of 2% of the VAT due, £176.38 (2% × £8,819) will arise. However, since the surcharge is less than £400 and calculated at either the 2% or the 5% rate, Customs will not collect this penalty. In addition, the surcharge period will be extended until 31.3.06.

(c) **The cash accounting scheme enables businesses to account for VAT on the basis of cash paid and received.** Thus under the scheme a trader achieves automatic bad debt relief since if the debtor does not pay, cash is not received and hence VAT is not accounted for. The date of payment or receipt determines the return in which the transaction is dealt with. **The scheme can only be used by a trader whose annual taxable turnover (exclusive of VAT) does not exceed £660,000.** A trader can join the scheme only if all returns and VAT payments are up to date (or arrangements have been made to pay outstanding VAT by instalments).

Marking guide

		Marks	
(a)	Output VAT on sales	1	
	Output VAT on advance payment	1	
	Scale charge	1	
	Expenses	1	
	Bad debts	2	
	Motor car	1	
			7
(b)	Issue surcharge liability notice	1	
	2% surcharge	1	
	Extension of surcharge period to 31.3.06	1	
			3
(c)	Turnover not exceeding £660,000	1	
	VAT returns and VAT payments up to date	1	
	Cash paid/received basis	1	
	Automatic bad debt relief	1	
	Tax point	1	
			5
			15

---

62   CHANDRA KHAN

> **Tutor's hint**. It was important to allocate your time carefully between the three distinct parts of this question.

(a)

	£
Deemed disposal proceeds (MV)	110,000
Less: cost	(38,000)
	72,000
Immediately chargeable (£75,000 – £38,000)	(37,000)
Gain held over by gift relief	35,000
Gain chargeable before taper relief	£37,000

The shares are a business asset that has been held for more than 2 years, so after taper relief 25% of the gain is chargeable.

Gain after taper relief (25% × £37,000)	£9,250

Tutorial notes

1   Deemed disposal proceeds equal the market value of the shares because Chandra's daughter is a connected person.

2   The amount immediately chargeable is the amount by which proceeds exceed allowable cost.

(b)

	£
Sale proceeds	146,000
Less: cost	(72,000)
Gain before taper relief	74,000
Business proportion (75%)	£55,500

As all of the proceeds of this proportion of the factory (£146,000 × 75% = £109,500) are reinvested in the new factory all of the £55,500 gain can be rolled over into the base cost of the new factory.

Gain on non business proportion (25%)	£18,500

This gain cannot be rolled over. However taper relief is due as the factory had been held for 6 years plus the additional year for non-business assets held before 6.4.98.

Gain after taper relief (75% × £18,500)	£13,875

(c)

	£
Disposal proceeds	100,000
Less: cost	-
Gain on incorporation	100,000

Shares	$\dfrac{200,000}{250,000} \times £100,000 =$	£80,000
Cash	$\dfrac{50,000}{250,000} \times £100,000 =$	£20,000

£20,000 of the gain is allocated to the cash consideration and is immediately chargeable.

As the business was owned for one complete year, 50% of this gain was chargeable after taper relief, ie £10,000.

Incorporation relief automatically rolls the gain allocated to the shares into the base cost of the shares for CGT purposes.

Marking guide

		Marks	
(a)	Deemed proceeds	1	
	Gain immediately chargeable	2	
	Gift relief	1	
	Gain after taper relief	1	
			5
(b)	Rollover relief	3	
	Gain immediately chargeable	1	
	Taper relief	1	
			5
(c)	Gain on goodwill	1	
	Allocation	1	
	Incorporation relief	1	
	Gain chargeable	1	
	Taper relief	1	
			5
			15

63   MR K

> **Tutor's hint.** It was important to spot that each of the motor cars was only available for part of the tax year and to time apportion the benefit accordingly.

(a) (i)   **Mercedes car**

		£
Car benefit £24,000 × 4/12 × 15%	1,200	
Fuel benefit £14,400 × 4/12 × 15%	720	
		1,920

Lexus car

Car benefit £36,000 × 6/12 × 25%	4,500	
Fuel benefit £14,400 × 6/12 × 25%	1,800	
		6,300

Legal costs and fine

Amount paid by company	1,200	
Less: contribution	(300)	
		900

(ii)   **Suits**

2 × £800 × 20%		320

(iii)   **Housing**

Annual rate	8,000	
Less: rent	(5,000)	
		3,000
Additional benefit		
(£125,000 - £75,000) × 5%		2,500
Total taxable benefits		14,940

(b)   **The company must pay Class 1A NICS at 12.8% in respect of all of the benefits provided to Mr K:**

12.8% × £14,940 = £1,912.32

(c)   MEMO
        To: Board of Q Ltd
        From: Certified accountant
        Date: 31 March 2005
        Subject: Annual cash bonuses to directors

The payment of cash bonuses to the directors will result in a Class 1 NIC charge for the company.

The director will be liable to income tax under PAYE on the bonus paid. If the director's other cash remuneration is below the Class 1 NIC earnings upper limit then he/she will be liable for Class 1 NIC at 11% until that limit is reached, and a further 1% on cash earnings above that limit.

Q Ltd will be responsible for collecting the director's PAYE and NIC due as well as accounting for its own NIC liability to the Revenue.

Any amounts of tax and national insurance contributions that Q Ltd is liable to deduct during each tax month ending on the 5th are due for payment to the Collector of Taxes not later than 14 days after the month ends, ie by the 19th of each month.

Employment income is taxed on the receipts basis. Thus the PAYE due will be collected on the date the bonus is deemed to be received by the director.

The time earnings are received is the earlier of:

(i)   The date of the actual payment of, or on account of, earnings, or
(ii)   The date an individual becomes entitled to such a payment.

However, in the case of directors, they are deemed to have received earnings on the earliest of potentially five dates which are the two dates already outlined plus the following three dates.

(iii) The date when sums on account of earnings are credited in the accounts

(iv)   The end of a period of account, where earnings are determined before the end of the period, and

(v)   The date when the amount of earnings for a period are determined if that is after the end of that period.

        Signed: Certified Accountant

Marking guide

		Marks	
(a)	**Mercedes car**		
	Car benefit	1	
	Fuel benefit	½	
	Lexus car		
	Car benefit	1	
	Fuel benefit	½	
	Legal costs	1	
	Suits	1	
	Housing	2	
			7
(b)			1
(c)	NICs	2	
	PAYE	2	
	Receipts basis	2	
	Due of receipt	1	
			7
			15

64   STRAIGHT PLC

> **Tutor's hint**. This was a fairly straightforward capital gains group question. If you are properly prepared, it should give you no trouble.

(a)   The companies form a capital gains group because:

    (i)   **At each level there is a 75% holding,** and
    (ii)   **Straight plc has an effective interest of over 50% in each of the companies.**

If Straight Ltd's holding in Arc Ltd were only 80%, Curve Ltd would not be in the group. This is because Straight Ltd's effective interest in Curve Ltd would be 48% (80% × 80% × 75%), (ie not over 50%).

(b)

	£	£
Schedule D Case I		185,000
Less: s 393(1) loss relief		(15,000)
		170,000
Capital gain (proceeds not reinvested)	80,000	
Less: capital loss	(10,000)	
		70,000
		240,000
Add: FII (£9,000 × 100/90)		10,000
		250,000

	£
CT @ 30% (W)	72,000
Less: small companies marginal relief	
11/400 (£375,000 – £250,000) × $\dfrac{240,000}{250,000}$	(3,300)
	68,700

Note. **Group dividends are not included in FII.**

(c)   An election for Straight plc to be treated as though it had sold Arc Ltd's freehold warehouse **must be made within two years of the end of the accounting period,** ie by **31.3.07**. The election may be beneficial as Straight plc would then be able to set the capital loss of £40,000 against its net gains of £70,000. Tax would consequently be saved on the £40,000 at the marginal rate of 32.5%.

Workings

1   *CT rate*

There are four associated companies so the small companies' upper and lower limits are:

Upper limit

$$\frac{£1,500,000}{4} = £375,000$$

Lower limit

$$\frac{£300,000}{4} = £75,000$$

∴ Small companies' marginal relief applies.

Marking guide

		Marks	
(a)	75% at each level	1	
	50% effective interest	1	
	Effect of reducing holding	2	
			4
(b)	Schedule DI	½	
	Loss relief	1	
	Net capital gain	3	
	FII	2	
	Corporation tax	1½	
			8
(c)	Time limit	1	
	Set of loss	1	
	Saving of marginal tax	1	
			3
			15

65 PETER, QUINTON AND ROGER

> **Tutor's hint**. In part (c) it was not sufficient to simply list the section numbers with no further detail.

(a) When a **partner joins a partnership the Schedule D Case I commencement rules apply to his share of partnership profits.**

(b) The profits of each period of account must initially be divided between the partners.

	Peter £	Quinton £	Roger £
Year to 31.12.02	20,000	20,000	
Year to 31.12.03	30,000	30,000	30,000
Year to 31.12.04	(10,000)	(10,000)	(10,000)

The assessments are:

	Peter £	Quinton £	Roger £
2001/02 (1.1.02 – 5.4.02)	5,000	5,000	-
2002/03 (y/e 31.12.02)/(1.1.03 – 5.4.03)	20,000	20,000	7,500
2003/04 (y/e 31.12.03)	30,000	30,000	30,000

(c) Peter, Quinton and Roger each have a Schedule D Case I trading loss of £10,000 in 2004/05.

Quinton and Roger can each carry their loss forward under s 385 ICTA 1988 to set against their future profits from the same trade. This relief is not available to Peter as he ceased trading on 31.12.04.

As Peter ceased trading in 2004/05, his loss of £10,000 is increased by his unrelieved overlap profits of £5,000.

Peter, Quinton and Roger can each claim to set their loss arising in 2004/05 against statutory total income in 2004/05 and/or in 2003/04 under s 380 ICTA 1988. Alternatively, they could each make a claim to set their 2004/05 loss against statutory total income in 2001/02, 2002/03 and 2003/04 in that order under s 381 ICTA 1988.

As Peter resigned in 2004/05, he could make a claim under s 388 ICTA 1988 to carry his loss back and set it against his Schedule D Case I profits in 2003/04, 2002/03 and 2001/02 in that order. Hence all of the loss would be relieved in 2003/04.

Marking scheme

		Marks	
(a)	Share of profits	1	
	Commencement rules	1	
			2
(b)	2001/02	2	
	2002/03 Peter and Quinton	1	
	Roger	2	
	2003/04	1	
			6
(c)	Loss allocated to each partner	2	
	S 385 ICTA 1988	1	
	S 380 ICTA 1988	1½	
	S 381 ICTA 1988	1½	
	S 388 ICTA 1988	1	
			7
			15

TAX RATES AND ALLOWANCES

A   INCOME TAX

1   *Rates*

	2004/05	
	£	%
Starting rate	1 – 2,020	10
Basic rate	2,021 – 31,400	22
Higher rate	34,401 and above	40

2   *Personal allowance*

	2004/05
	£
Personal allowance	4,745

3   *Cars – 2004/05*

Base level of CO_2 emissions – 145g/km

4   *Car fuel charge – 2004/05*

Base figure £14,400

5   *Personal pension contribution limits*

Age	Maximum percentage %
Up to 35	17.5
36 – 45	20.0
46 – 50	25.0
51 – 55	30.0
56 – 60	35.0
61 or more	40.0

Subject to earnings cap of £102,000 for 2004/05.

Maximum contribution without evidence of earnings £3,600.

6   *Capital allowances*

	%
Plant and machinery	
Writing down allowance★	25
First year allowance★★	40
First year allowance (information and communication technology equipment until 31.3.04, low emission cars (CO_2 emissions of less than 120 g/km))	100
Industrial buildings allowance	4

★ 6% reducing balance for certain long life assets

★★ 50% for small enterprises between 1.4.04 – 31.3.05 (6.4.04 – 5.4.05 for unincorporated businesses)

B   CORPORATION TAX

1   *Rates*

Financial year	2002	2003	2004
Starting rate	Nil	Nil	Nil
Small companies rate	19%	19%	19%
Full rate	30%	30%	30%
	£	£	£
Starting rate lower limit	10,000	10,000	10,000
Starting rate upper limit	50,000	50,000	50,000
Small companies rate lower limit	300,000	300,000	300,000
Small companies rate upper limit	1,500,000	1,500,000	1,500,000
Taper relief fraction			
Starting rate	19/400	19/400	19/400
Small companies rate	11/400	11/400	11/400

From 1.4.04 profits paid out as dividends are subject to minimum rate of CT of 19%

2   *Marginal relief*

$(M - P) \times I/P \times$ Marginal relief fraction

C   VALUE ADDED TAX

Registration and deregistration limits

Registration limit	£58,000
Deregistration limit	£56,000
VAT on private petrol – quarterly scale charge	
CC of car: 1400cc or less	232
Over 1400cc up to 2000cc	293
Over 2000cc	432

D   RATES OF INTEREST

Official rate of interest: 5% (assumed)

Rate of interest on unpaid tax: 6.5% (assumed)

Rate of interest on overpaid tax: 2.5% (assumed)

REVIEW FORM & FREE PRIZE DRAW

All original review forms from the entire BPP range, completed with genuine comments, will be entered into one of two draws on 31 July 2005 and 31 January 2006. The names on the first four forms picked out on each occasion will be sent a cheque for £50.

Name: _____   Address: _____

_____

_____

How have you used this Kit?
(Tick one box only)

☐ Self study (book only)

☐ On a course: college (please state)_____

_____

☐ With 'correspondence' package

☐ Other _____

Why did you decide to purchase this Kit? *(Tick one box only)*

☐ Have used the complementary Study Text

☐ Have used other BPP products in the past

☐ Recommendation by friend/colleague

☐ Recommendation by a lecturer at college

☐ Saw advertising in journals

☐ Saw website

☐ Other _____

During the past six months do you recall seeing/receiving any of the following?
(Tick as many boxes as are relevant)

☐ Our advertisement in *Student Accountant*

☐ Our advertisement in *Pass*

☐ Our brochure with a letter through the post

☐ Our website

Which (if any) aspects of our advertising do you find useful?
(Tick as many boxes as are relevant)

☐ Prices and publication dates of new editions

☐ Information on product content

☐ Facility to order books off-the-page

☐ None of the above

When did you sit the exam? _____

Which BPP products have you used?

Text	☐	**MCQ cards**	☐	**i-Learn**	☐
Kit	☑	**Tape**	☐	**i-Pass**	☐
Passcard	☐	**Success CD**	☐	**Virtual Campus**	☐

Your ratings, comments and suggestions would be appreciated on the following areas of this Kit.

	Very useful	Useful	Not useful
Effective revision	☐	☐	☐
Exam guidance	☐	☐	☐
Websites and mindmaps	☐	☐	☐
Paper-based examination questions	☐	☐	☐
Content and structure of answers	☐	☐	☐
Mock exams	☐	☐	☐
Mock exam answers	☐	☐	☐

	Excellent	Good	Adequate	Poor
Overall opinion of this Kit	☐	☐	☐	☐

Do you intend to continue using BPP products?   ☐ Yes   ☐ No

Please note any further comments and suggestions/errors on the reverse of this page. The BPP author of this edition can be e-mailed at: SueDexter@bpp.com

Please return this form to: Catherine Watton, ACCA range manager, BPP Professional Education, FREEPOST, London, W12 8BR

REVIEW FORM & FREE PRIZE DRAW (continued)

Please note any further comments and suggestions/errors below.

FREE PRIZE DRAW RULES

1   Closing date for 31 July 2005 draw is 30 June 2005. Closing date for 31 January 2006 draw is 31 December 2005.

2   Restricted to entries with UK and Eire addresses only. BPP employees, their families and business associates are excluded.

3   No purchase necessary. Entry forms are available upon request from BPP Professional Education. No more than one entry per title, per person. Draw restricted to persons aged 16 and over.

4   Winners will be notified by post and receive their cheques not later than 6 weeks after the relevant draw date.

5   The decision of the promoter in all matters is final and binding. No correspondence will be entered into.

See overleaf for information on other
BPP products and how to order

ACCA Order

To BPP Professional Education, Aldine Place, London W12 8AW
Tel: 020 8740 2211
Fax: 020 8740 1184
email: publishing@bpp.com
website: www.bpp.com
Order online www.bpp.com

Mr/Mrs/Ms (Full name)

Daytime delivery address

Postcode

Daytime Tel

Date of exam (month/year)   Scots law variant Y / N

Occasionally we may wish to email you relevant offers and information about courses and products. Please tick to opt into this service. ☐

	6/04 Texts	1/05 Kits	1/05 Passcards	***Success CDs	8/04 i-Learn	8/04 i-Pass	Virtual Campus
PART 1							
1.1 Preparing Financial Statements UK	£24.95	£12.95	£9.95	£14.95	£34.95	£24.95	£90
1.2 Financial Information for Management	£24.95	£12.95	£9.95	£14.95	£34.95	£24.95	£90
1.3 Managing People	£24.95	£12.95	£9.95	£14.95	£34.95	£24.95	£90
PART 2							
2.1 Information Systems	£24.95	£12.95	£9.95	£14.95	£34.95	£24.95	£90
2.2 Corporate and Business Law UK **	£24.95†	£12.95	£9.95	£14.95	£34.95	£24.95	£90
2.3 Business Taxation FA2004	£24.95†	£12.95	£9.95	£14.95	£34.95	£24.95	£90
2.4 Financial Management and Control	£24.95	£12.95	£9.95	£14.95	£34.95	£24.95	£90
2.5 Financial Reporting UK (7/04)	£24.95	£12.95	£9.95	£14.95	£34.95	£24.95	£90
2.6 Audit and Internal Review UK	£24.95	£12.95	£9.95	£14.95	£34.95	£24.95	£90
PART 3							
3.1 Audit and Assurance Services UK	£24.95	£12.95	£9.95	£14.95		£24.95	
3.2 Advanced Taxation FA2004	£24.95†	£12.95	£9.95	£14.95		£24.95	
3.3 Performance Management	£24.95	£12.95	£9.95	£14.95		£24.95	
3.4 Business Information Management	£24.95	£12.95	£9.95	£14.95		£24.95	
3.5 Strategic Business Planning and Development	£24.95	£12.95	£9.95	£14.95		£24.95	
3.6 Advanced Corporate Reporting UK (7/04)	£24.95	£12.95	£9.95	£14.95		£24.95	
3.7 Strategic Financial Management	£24.95	£12.95	£9.95	£14.95		£24.95	
INTERNATIONAL STREAM							
1.1 Preparing Financial Statements (Int'l)	£24.95	£12.95	£9.95		£34.95	£24.95	
2.2 Corporate and Business Law (Global)	£24.95	£12.95	£9.95			£24.95	
2.5 Financial Reporting (Int'l)	£24.95	£12.95	£9.95		£34.95	£24.95	
2.6 Audit and Internal Review (Int'l)	£24.95	£12.95	£9.95		£34.95	£24.95	
3.1 Audit and Assurance Services (Int'l)	£24.95	£12.95	£9.95				
3.6 Advanced Corporate Reporting (Int'l)	£24.95	£12.95	£9.95				
Success in Your Research and Analysis							
Project - Tutorial Text (10/04)	£24.95						
Learning to Learn (7/02)	£9.95						

† (**8/04** for 6/05 & 12/05 exams)

SUBTOTAL £ ☐

POSTAGE & PACKING

Study Texts

	First	Each extra	Online
UK	£5.00	£2.00	£2.00
Europe*	£6.00	£4.00	£4.00
Rest of world	£20.00	£10.00	£10.00

Kits

	First	Each extra	Online
UK	£5.00	£2.00	£2.00
Europe*	£6.00	£4.00	£4.00
Rest of world	£20.00	£10.00	£10.00

Passcards/Success Tapes/CDs

	First	Each extra	Online
UK	£2.00	£1.00	£1.00
Europe*	£3.00	£2.00	£2.00
Rest of world	£8.00	£8.00	£8.00

Grand Total (incl. Postage) £

I enclose a cheque for
(Cheques to *BPP Professional Education*)

Or charge to Visa/Mastercard/Switch

Card Number

Expiry date   Start Date

Issue Number (Switch Only)

Signature

We aim to deliver to all UK addresses inside 5 working days; a signature will be required. Orders to all EU addresses should be delivered within 6 working days. All other orders to overseas addresses should be delivered within 8 working days. * Europe includes the Republic of Ireland and the Channel Islands. ** For Scots law variant students, a free **Scots Law Supplement** is available with the 2.2 Text. Please indicate in the name and address section if this applies to you. ***Alternatively, Success Tapes are available for the same papers, all £12.95.